Families
on the move

Acknowledgements

My thanks go to Dr David Pollock whose heart and work for TCKs has inspired me, and to the families of Arab World Ministries whose lives have enriched my own.

Dedication

To my own family – Bryan, my constant source of encouragement, and three great kids, Russell, Matthew and Kirstin.

Families
on the move

Growing up overseas— and *loving it!*

Marion Knell

MONARCH
B O O K S
MILL HILL, LONDON & GRAND RAPIDS, MICHIGAN

First published by Monarch Books in the UK in 2001,
Concorde House, Grenville Place, Mill Hill, London NW7 3SA.

Published by Monarch Books in the USA in 2001.

Illustrated by Bridget Gillespie

Distributed by:
UK: STL, PO Box 300, Kingstown Broadway,
Carlisle, Cumbria CA3 0QS;
USA: Kregel Publications, PO Box 2607,
Grand Rapids, Michigan 49501.

ISBN 1 85424 523 6 (UK)
ISBN 0 8254 6018 2 (USA)

British Library Cataloguing Data
A catalogue record for this book is available from the British Library.

emis

Published in conjunction with EMIS, Billy Graham Center, Wheaton
College, Illinois 60187-5593, USA.

Designed and produced for the publisher by
Gazelle Creative Productions,
Concorde House, Grenville Place, Mill Hill,
London NW7 3SA.

Contents

 Foreword

A bout twenty years ago I got married. To a nurse. To a good-looking nurse! And, to get to the point, to a good-looking nurse from the good old U. S. of A. It was a crash course in cultural confusion. We got hung up on curtains and 'drapes'. She put the shopping in the 'trunk' – did we own an elephant? – I put it in the boot.

Pancakes for breakfast, peanut butter and jelly sandwiches. . . my stomach had to apply for an American visa!

And all this fuss because two 'first-world' citizens were learning to live together.

So what happens when the 'first world' meets the 'two-thirds' world'? When you are coping with a new language, different climate, alien customs and a bad case of jet lag, exactly what do you do?

Marion Knell has done the church a great service by examining how families survive as they move around the global village. She explores the impact of trans-continental mobility, examining its effects in the lives of children, teenagers. . . and their parents!

Families on the Move will add to our understanding of overseas missionaries and ex-pats working abroad. It should be read by pastors of churches, as well as every missionary personnel department and candidate. It will also prove valuable to diplomats, military families, businessmen and women – indeed anyone crossing cultural boundaries. And it should especially be read by my aunt Phyllis who thinks everywhere in the world is just like Britain only hotter!

As for me, I'm going to recommend Marion's book to all my globe-trotting friends. . . just as soon as I've finished devouring my dessert of Mississippi mud pie!

Stephen Gaukroger
Gold Hill Baptist Church, Gerrards Cross, Bucks, UK

▶ Introduction

If…

You can't answer the question 'Where are you from?'…

Someone brings up the name of a team and you get the sport wrong…

Fitting fifteen or more people into a car seems normal to you…

…the chances are you're a TCK – a Third Culture Kid or Trans-Culture Kid. 'TCK' is the term used to describe anyone from anywhere who has spent time growing up overseas.

This book is written for those families currently living overseas, those contemplating such a move and those who are trying to digest the implications of having lived overseas. In our very mobile world, shrinking every moment with e-mail, internet and satellite communications, we are constantly encountering other cultures, crossing cultural bridges and re-examining our cultural identity.

It is also intended for those working in the personnel departments of organisations with overseas postings. Employees or members with families are likely to stay in their postings much longer and function more effectively if the needs of the whole family have been addressed and if adequate preparation has been given to them before embarking on the experience.

Being a TCK is a lifetime experience. You don't stop being a TCK when you reach 18. In the past, organisations have spent time and money preparing their representatives for life abroad but have paid scant attention to the implications of major moves for the whole family and especially for children. Children have been left without a voice in the process and without the necessary tools to handle the changes and incorporate what they have learnt into their total life experience.

Relatives and friends of families going overseas also benefit from knowing what to expect. Many are anxious about the possible effects of prolonged separation and want to know what they can do to maintain contact and keep the relationship alive. In the case of charity and aid workers, they may have a commitment to support the family whilst overseas and need guidance on the best ways of doing this.

So, how can we prepare our children and ourselves for this 'lifetime experience'? What are the issues involved and the long-term implications? What about living in another culture? What should we be aware of or beware of? What strategies can we put in place not just to cope but to maximise the benefits of the experience? What are the educational considerations and implications? How can we prepare children for re-entry into their home culture? What problems are they likely to face?

These are the issues this book sets out to explore. It is not just a 'how-to' book. As well as setting out the agenda, the intention is to give the reader, the individual family, the stimulus to work through the issues for themselves.

Finally, I would like to champion the cause of those bringing children up overseas – it's a marvellous experience and opportunity. Today's TCKs are the culture-brokers of the twenty-first century. They will make it possible to build bridges across the cultural divides that the rest of us have to struggle with. They have a panoramic window on the world through which we can glimpse the world in its richness and diversity. It's OK to be a TCK!

Chapter 1

Third Culture Kids

Ten ways to know you're a Third Culture Kid:

1. You consider a city 500km away to be 'very close'.
2. You wince when people mispronounce foreign words.
3. You bargain with the shopkeeper.
4. You sort your friends by continent.
5. You speak with authority on the subject of airline travel.
6. You can cut grass with a machete but can't start a lawnmower.
7. You watch the latest film and miss the subtitles.
8. You read *National Geographic* and recognise someone.
9. You speak two languages but can't spell either.
10. You have friends from or in twenty-nine different countries.

A shrinking world, the demands of global communications and the greater flexibility in the job market has meant that now, more than ever before, people are working and taking their families to countries with which they have no natural affinity. Out of this has grown a new community – that of the Third Culture Kid or Trans-Culture Kid. TCKs are to be found everywhere – in the armed forces, the multi-national corporations, the diplomatic community and the missions community. More and more people are going overseas to study or to do research, and they take their families with them.

The implications of growing up overseas are enormous and need to be understood in order to make maximum use of the experience. It will be easy for some children, difficult for others. There are many variables in the experience which will determine the effects it has, including the location, the age of the child, the length of stay, and, not least, the child's own personality.

Unfortunately, inadequate preparation is too often given to those moving overseas both before they go and upon their return. Being a TCK is not something one grows out of – it is a lifetime experience.

So, what goes into making a TCK? A typical 12-year-old TCK commented: 'I'm always considered a foreigner wherever I live.'

The TCK profile

Dave Pollock, who has worked with TCKs for many years in the United States, has produced what is now the classic definition of a TCK:

> A TCK is an individual who, having spent a significant part of the developmental years in a culture other than the parents' culture, develops a sense of relationship to all of the cultures while not having full ownership of any. Elements from each culture are incorporated into the life experience, but the sense of belonging is in relationship to others of similar experience.[1]

That definition itself raises a number of questions. How long is 'significant'? What is meant by 'developmental years'? What does the phrase 'full ownership' mean?

The period of a child's life between birth and the age of 18 is referred to as the 'developmental years'. This is the time during which a child's sense of identity, world view, relationships and allegiances are formed. Whilst living overseas affects everyone to some extent, whether they are young or old, the difference for a child is that this is when core aspects of its personality and value system are being formed. A child cannot view the experience as objectively as an adult can. Subconsciously, it is absorbing the influences of the cultures with which it is surrounded.

What is a significant amount of time? It must be borne in mind that, given the short span of a child's lifetime, the word 'significant' will apply to a shorter spell than it would to an adult. Generally in this context the phrase means spending two years or more in a mobile, multi-cultural setting. Together with the time factor, one must consider the depth of the child's involvement in the culture, or cultures, the parental attitude to the situation and the host country's attitude to outsiders. All of these affect the long-term impact of living overseas.

The question of 'ownership' refers to the sense of belonging – how do you answer the question 'Where do you come from?' Faced with a multiplicity of cultures, the parents', the host country, the expatriate community, the school culture, a TCK finds himself being pulled many ways and yet belonging nowhere. He identifies in some measure with each of them but does not find a secure niche in any. The problem comes down to that of roots – 'Where is home?'

Because there is no sense of belonging to any one culture, the TCK 'incorporates' elements from each culture into his own personality and life experience. He adopts values (political, religious, and economic), perspectives (on life, history, and society) and tastes (relating to food, clothing, music, humour, and literature), from each culture in which he has been immersed and 'incorporates' them into his life experience. In the course of several moves such elements may be gathered from very diverse cultures in different parts of the world.

To sum up, the first culture is the home culture of the parents. In the case of cross-cultural marriage this will be two cultures. Where step-families are involved the number may be more. The second is the host culture, the culture of the country of residence. Where several moves are made it will encompass all the host cultures. The third culture is the community of people who have the shared experience of growing up in two cultures. It is not just the blending of the first two cultures. TCKs have something in common with each other no matter where they grew up and no matter in what circumstances.

Most of my work has been with families working for charities overseas. However, I was talking with a former student of mine about my work with TCKs and she suddenly exclaimed, 'But that's me! I understand what you're talking about completely. My father was with the RAF and we spent my whole childhood moving around the world. I thought no-one understood, but you've just made sense of it for me!'

Put a crowd of TCKs from all over the world together in a room and there will be an immediate buzz – no introductions or explanations will be necessary!

TCKs, then, have more in common with each other than with their mono-cultural peers, wherever they may be from. This has major implications for TCKs returning home to study at tertiary education level. For them there is a sense of being a foreigner in one's country of passport and a need to explain how and why they feel different even though they look as though they belong.

On the positive side, the global marketplace and growth of multi-national companies make greater demands for people with language and cross-cultural skills. TCKs have proved to be and will continue to be very significant in the world of business, foreign affairs and diplomacy, as people who can bridge cultures, who are 'culture-brokers'. Henry Luce, who co-founded *Time* magazine, grew up in China, the son of missionary parents. TCKs should be encouraged to make use of the experience of being overseas and the lessons they have learned. In making moves they develop skills that will last a lifetime in the future changes they may make.

The experience can also be a lot of fun. When asked what he enjoyed about life in Japan, Nathan replied, 'The change of scenery, the food, the different cultures, the people in Japan being so polite and welcoming, learning the language, the skiing, the school, the countryside, sport, music… ! I learnt about different people and had another perspective on life.'

The issues

Parents who want to help their children cope with this process need to increase their level of awareness of what is going on so that they can prepare for it, at both a personal and community level. Children need to be properly prepared to cope with the experience and helped along the way to process what is happening to them. The company responsible for the assignment, the extended family, the local support network, and the home church, should all be educated on the TCK profile and the implications it has for child and parents.

I want to look at some of the main issues raised. Bringing up a family overseas presents many challenges but these do not have to be viewed as problem areas. With a good grasp of what makes up the TCK experience, strategies can be put in place to cope with those challenges and create a sound basis on which to build for the future.

Mobility

On average, a TCK makes eight major moves before he/she is 18. Two major moves occur each time the family comes 'home' and returns overseas or to a new location. Difficulties are foreseen when going to a new culture, but are often not expected when returning home. The assumption is made that the family is returning to familiar territory. But for children who have grown up overseas, nothing about it is familiar. It holds no memories or landmarks. Even for adults, places and people change with astounding speed. The years go by more quickly as one gets older. Someone said they felt like they were riding a bike uphill all the way to 30; after that it was downhill all the way so fast there was no way to slow down. For a child, a year is a significant amount of time.

There are benefits to mobility. TCKs tend to be adaptable, flexible, confident in change – they have done it before and it has worked, so change is not something to be feared. They learn to travel light, to know how to make a good start quickly and to know the importance of people rather than places or things.

They have a rich memory bank of all the places they've been to and experiences they've enjoyed. While their mono-cultural peers have been watching soaps on TV, they've been on the airstrips, in the desert, meeting people from all over the world, learning other ways of living, other values. They have been in the places where news is made.

I asked one TCK to tell me a story from his time overseas. He replied: 'Which story do you want? The deadly snake-bite story, the tear gas in the school patio story or the bomb blast blowing glass out all over my bed while I was asleep story?'

Roots

The challenge of mobility lies in finding and defining one's roots. For TCKs home is always 'elsewhere'. They can fit in anywhere, but belong nowhere. Geographically rootless TCKs find their roots not in places but in people, in relationships. For them, home is wherever their parents are, even if they themselves have never lived there. It is the family relationship which gives them stability. In chapter two we shall be looking at how to provide for and nourish that relationship.

Because of the constant moving around, TCKs often develop a migratory instinct – they soon get itchy feet after being in any one place for a time. This can affect their academic life, career, family and marriage. Many experience a longing for stability in their lives, a sense of permanence. This may lead them to seek a partner with a more settled background, a real home-loving person who has never moved from the town where they were born, only to discover after a few years that they find it difficult themselves to settle down long-term in one place. Rebecca said: 'I developed strategies for establishing myself in groups, but still have problems with attachment.'

Similarly, decision-making can be a problem – settling to one course of study or action, to one relationship, to one contract for a period of time, anything which involves long-term commitment or looking far into the future. Many TCKs themselves end up overseas either in a short-term capacity, such as voluntary work before or after university, or long-term in employment. This is not necessarily in the area where they grew up or in the same profession in which their parents were employed. In many cases this highlights the positive way they feel about having lived overseas. For some it is a kind of nomadic wandering, in search of a place to belong but never staying long enough to find it.

Adaptability is a great asset – but when does it

become one move too many for children? We say children are resilient, they bounce back. But like the rubber band, sometimes the strain becomes too great and the elastic snaps. Being a TCK sometimes feels like the extreme sports version of bungee-jumping! There are occasions when, for the good of the children, it is necessary to refuse certain assignments, another move. Being a TCK is a lifetime experience. No-one wants it to be a lifetime of putting the pieces back together again.

Relationships

TCKs have a very rich relationship bank of all the people they have met and known and shared their lives with. The people they go to school with, the people amongst whom they live, the people their parents work with, local dignitaries may all form the social network of the TCK. Many of these, too, will also be highly mobile. Whilst the individual TCK may be moving every year or two years, his school friends, maybe from many different countries, will be doing the same, and not necessarily at the same time. So you arrive, make friends, your best friend goes off in six months, arrives back three months later and three months after that you're on the move again.

The plus side of this is that TCKs recognise the importance of 'now'– if you don't make friends now, it may be too late. So a typical first meeting between two TCKs may start like this:

'Who are you?'

'Where are you from?'

'How long are you staying?'

TCKS are very good at initiating relationships, making the first move. When they return home, they can be the people who will make things happen because they have experience in taking control of situations.

The challenge is that TCKs may have made too many

relationships and be unwilling to commit themselves long-term. Reactions can range from the 'absence makes the heart grow fonder' kind, where TCKs develop a large network of friends, run up huge phone bills, are forever writing letters, or, more likely now, tie up the email line, to the 'out of sight, out of mind' kind, where the hold on a relationship is released rather too easily. With all the changes, TCKs may have difficulty in long-term planning, because the future has never been sure.

Richard says:

I have friends all around the world now and I never really want to settle in one place for the rest of my life. One effect of moving around so much is that I have found it hard in the friendships that I develop to be committed beyond a certain point. I think that in general I have a real problem with commitment as I am always prepared to move on to another place.

Leave-taking

Because of the number of moves TCKs make, leave-taking is a major feature in their lives. If they learn to do it well, it will be an invaluable skill in later life. It is accepted that the manner in which you leave one situation determines how well you will enter the next. For adults and children it is important to know how to handle this area. We'll be thinking more about it when we look at Transition and Re-entry. For now, I just want to say that TCKs need to be helped to say goodbye in ways that are appropriate to them and the people they are leaving behind, to know how to be reconciled to situations and people and how to express the grief they feel for what is past and lost to them. In learning how to say goodbye properly, TCKs develop empathy and sensitivity for others.

The challenge comes in giving children the time and

It had become necessary to start on the Christmas cards
no later than March.

space to grieve and make farewells. It is a mistake to hurry children home. If grief is not appropriately expressed at the time it is experienced, it can surface at a later date and be much more intense. The subject of coping with grief will be looked at in chapter three. Because uprooting and leaving is a painful experience, TCKs may be wary of too great a degree of intimacy. They may put up the barriers to anyone getting very close to them; they are vulnerable when it comes to making firm commitments in relationships. However, having made a commitment, when difficulties arise, they may let go of the relationship too easily because letting go is such a normal part of their life history.

Language

TCKs can usually speak at least two languages, sometimes three, particularly if the parents are from different language groups. Whilst this may be the norm in many parts of Europe, in England and America it certainly is not. Children learn languages much more easily than adults do, mainly because they are less self-conscious about the process. The way we speak is a key to the way we think and behave. Learning the language of the host country is a good way to identify with the emotions and culture of the people of that country. It enables the child to cope and communicate in the new country.

The challenge is that sometimes the mother tongue is never properly mastered, particularly if the child has to attend a school for which the language medium is neither his/her own mother tongue nor the language of the host country. Working in more than one language can lead to confusion and learning difficulties because it means adopting two patterns of thought concepts. We will be looking at that further in chapter seven.

World perspective

TCKs know the world does not end at the border or the channel or the sea. They are great at seeing the other side of the question. National press carries its own bias, but the TCK sees the news it reports through another cultural lens. They read about the events but can hear the sounds, smell the smells, know the emotion behind the stories. They have seen the floods, the droughts, heard the gunfire, watched the flames. In many ways they show greater maturity in life because they have broader horizons and wider experience of the world. Theirs is a greater realism, based on coping with loss and learning to adapt.

Richard again says:

> I loved the climate and food. I loved travelling and seeing new things and living in exciting new places. It was all a fantastic adventure that I never wanted to stop. I loved the fact that I'd seen so many places people only see on TV. I think my life is much richer for having been overseas, I've seen so much and experienced so many cultures.

However, some TCKs grow up in very protected environments, such as on expatriate compounds or in boarding schools. Many overseas cultures are more conservative than the home culture. For this reason, some TCKs never go through the irresponsibility and experimentation associated with adolescence. Whilst parents at the time may breathe a sigh of relief, a period of delayed adolescence can occur later on in life when there is a desire to throw off restraints and defy convention. The problem is that by this time the TCK may have commitments which make such behaviour very difficult to accommodate.

The clash of cultures

Culture expresses itself in what we do, what we say,

the customs and traditions we follow. Underneath those outward expressions of culture lie the internal workings, what we believe, our values and assumptions about ourselves and the world in which we live, the way we think. It is quite interesting to compare TCKs to immigrant communities, many of which assume the practices of their adopted countries – but underneath that surface conformity, there remains an entrenched loyalty to the values and beliefs of their mother culture. Similarly, whilst physically looking very much like their national counterparts in their home culture, TCKs may feel very differently about themselves underneath.

Returning TCKs tend to be very judgemental of their own culture, seeing its deficiencies in the light of everything else they have experienced. Such views, when vigorously expressed, may be regarded as 'unpatriotic'. They may also feel divided loyalties when it comes to national allegiance – when the World Cup football begins and England plays Tunisia, or France the Cameroons, whom should they support?

TCKs need to find a cultural balance. As we have seen, as well as the two main cultures, they are exposed to various sub-cultures. In some countries the expatriate culture is quite strong, yet bears little relationship to the home culture. Similarly, the school culture may be that of a bygone colonial era or of another country altogether. Moving from one host country to another means that the rules of conduct change and the TCK has to relearn the way to play the game. On returning 'home', he has to find a balance with which he can feel comfortable, retain his integrity and yet find acceptance in the community to which he returns.

Dr Ted Ward in his article 'The MK's Advantage: Three Cultural Contexts' says:

Notice the frequency of the word 'survive' in reference to cultural living... Every time you hear the word survive replace

The problems caused by divided loyalties.

Families on the Move

it with the word thrive. Because growing up overseas gives the flexibility of intercultural experience, the concrete awareness of what the world is really like and the multi-lingual and international experience, TCKs are well-equipped to cope in today's marketplace.[2]

In other words, it's OK to be a TCK!

Questions

These are directed towards parents taking a family overseas. Adult TCKs should answer them for themselves.

1. How many moves has your child made? How did he/she react?
2. At what point in the child's life cycle were those moves made? At what point in the life cycle will the next move occur?
3. Where do you perceive the family's long-term roots to be? If you were evacuated suddenly, where would you return to?
4. In what areas do you think your child/children might particularly struggle with the TCK experience?
5. Do you personally know any other TCKs to whom you could talk about the experience?
6. What is your own attitude to going overseas and being uprooted? What message are you giving your child, either verbally or non-verbally?

Notes

1. *The Third Culture Kid Experience* by David C. Pollock and Ruth E. Van Reken, published by Intercultural Press 1999.
2. *The MK's Advantage: Three Cultural Contexts*: a presentation given at ICMK Quito, January 1987.

I <u>RECOMMEND</u> the TCK lifestyle BECAUSE...IT'S OK

I DON'T RECOMMEND IT... SOMETIMES

▶ Chapter 2

Building a Firm Foundation

I f it is true that, for TCKs, roots lie in relationships, not in places, then it is of primary importance to their well-being and stability that the relationship in which they find their roots be well nourished. For parents this raises two fundamental questions:

1. How can we nurture our relationship as husband and wife?
2. How can we ensure a healthy platform for our family?

Finding an answer to the first may be additionally complicated by the nature of the host country's society. It may not be possible to do the 'normal' things you do as a couple back home to relax and restore yourselves away from the children. More attention will be given to this when considering life in a non-Western society.

General perspectives

In thinking about the second question, our perception of what constitutes a 'healthy family platform' may be coloured by our own experiences as children and the examples of parent-modelling to which we have been exposed. The following outline of generational perspectives may help to clarify this for the parents reading this or the people for whom the reader is responsible.

The Baby Boomers

This refers to the group born between 1946 and 1964. For them, self-fulfilment is very important as well as economic affluence. Their early adult years were spent against a backdrop of material prosperity, good education, good employment prospects and some generally accepted values. They manage a career and family together, sometimes at the expense of family nurture. This group has seen a rise in the divorce rate and in fragmented, dysfunctional families. Individualism is highly prized, there is less emphasis on sacrifice than their parents had and more concern for the best for themselves at whatever stage they may be. This attitude affects decisions made regarding families as well.

As a consequence there is less commitment – if a relationship or job does not work, then they tend to move on. Most traditional values and norms have been discarded but there is a high degree of idealism, seen with regard to concern for the environment and civil rights issues. This generation tends to be very activity-led, and although there is supposed to be more time for leisure, that time is eaten up by all the other things they want to do, to achieve, to be involved in. All of this impacts on family dynamics and expectations.

The Busters or 'Generation X'

'Generation X' is a title coined from a book of the same name by Douglas Copeland and describes the last generation to reach adulthood in the twentieth century. This has been described as the most indulged and most neglected generation in recent history. Indulged because they have had more material goods, but neglected because of increasing family fragmentation, domestic violence, sexual abuse and drug dependence. They feel abandoned and alienated, hungry for a reality that the plastic world they live in doesn't offer. Many have poor parental role models and low self-esteem. Moreover the message from the media is 'If it's good, go with it, if it's not – get out.' Marriage, or long-term commitment, may be seen as an ideal, but one which is unattainable.

Against a background of low employment, inability to use their skills, lack of community and poor family relationships, Generation Xers are nevertheless looking for truth, reality and absolutes and will not stand any superficial or easy answers. They have grown up with the 'sound-bite' and modern marketing techniques which lead to distrust. They take longer to get married or form lasting partnerships, to establish careers and to start a family. Lack of jobs and the move to short-term contracts reinforces the instability they feel.

This is the first generation to have used computers as children. David F. Wells in his book 'God in the Wasteland' says: 'Our computers are starting to talk to us, while our neighbours are becoming more distant and anonymous.'[1]

For this generation in particular the need to provide the opportunity for acquiring good skills in relationships and parenting is paramount. Many are determined to do a better job than their parents but because of their own needs are often less able to focus on the needs of others.

A healthy family platform

I would like to suggest Dr Marjorie Foyle's outline of a healthy family platform as a good place to start.[2]

Caring and love

This probably sounds obvious, but many of the families
going overseas come from Generation X. Consistency,
stability and conflict resolution have not been the hallmark of
their upbringing and though the extended family may be very
large, with several step-parent and step-sibling relationships,
it may not be very close. If you recognised yourself in that
description, then be assured that there are ways of learning
the skills, and the fact that you may have had poor role
models as parents is not an insuperable obstacle to being a
good parent yourself. Someone once said to me, 'Your child
doesn't want a perfect parent, they need *you*.'

The sort of caring and love on which a healthy family
is based is unconditional. It is love which can be relied upon
in the face of adversity, it loves in spite of the conduct of
individuals. When overseas, parents often do not have access
to role-modelling, older people who have been through the
difficulties they are currently encountering with their
children. They have no-one to turn to for advice and
support, no-one to tell them that they are doing fine and to
persevere or to ease up on things. Even with the best
possible motives things can go wrong, but to have the child's
best interests at heart is a very good place to begin.

Consistent discipline

If there is one area that is likely to cause tension
between different families, it's the question of discipline. All
parents have their own ideas about what is or is not

acceptable behaviour. The important thing for their children is that they know where the boundaries lie. For that assurance, discipline needs to be consistent and predictable. When a parent says one thing and then does another, the child has no idea where the boundaries are – and children feel secure with boundaries.

How often have you been in the check-out queue at the supermarket and seen the child in front ask for sweets, demand sweets, whine for sweets, cry, lie on the floor and scream for sweets? The mother says no on the first three occasions and then finally gives in. What has the child learnt? Make enough fuss and you get your own way – until Mum is provoked too far and loses control.

Discipline needs to be comprehensible to the child. Sitting down and explaining the consequences of certain actions makes the rules easier to accept. As a child grows older, those rules need to be amended, in consultation with the child. There is no cause to be rigid but it is essential to be regular, dependable. Rules can always be relaxed for special reasons.

Having a well-defined family code of discipline is especially valuable in cross-cultural situations. Working, living alongside and mixing with people of very different cultural, social and ethnic backgrounds can be quite stressful for a family. Having children to stay, or allowing one's own children to go to others' homes, is made easier if there are clearly understood ground rules for behaviour. Parents need to respect those guidelines in each other's homes and to endeavour not to criticise them.

Communication

Because both parents and children spend a lot of their time watching screens of one sort or another, there is a need to rediscover and develop the art of communication. The first rule is to master the art of listening. We all know how

David's mother had found an effective strategy for getting
past the sweet display.

infuriating it is to pour out our hearts to someone only for them to say 'What was that you were saying?' There are certain basic dos and don'ts when it comes to listening to children:

Do...
- Set aside other things.
- Comfort – take it seriously.
- Respond – make the sort of noises that show you understand.
- Watch your face – don't look horrified, even if you feel it.
- Inform them of the real state of affairs, especially if they're fearful.
- Be positive about the situation.
- Watch their behaviour, their non-verbal communication.
- Check the other side's story before acting.

Don't...
- Laugh at them or their fears.
- Ignore what they're trying to tell you.
- Over-react to what you're told.
- Criticise their feelings.
- Interrupt them.
- Compare them to their siblings.
- Say 'I'm too busy.'
- Embarrass them in front of others.

Prior to going overseas, children may have fears that are very real to them even though they seem laughable to parents. It is vital that they feel free to express these fears without being ridiculed or criticised. Daniel was in tears when he heard his house had been sold. He seemed quite inconsolable. When his mother probed deeper, he revealed his fear: 'Shall we have to live in a tent forever now?' A look at some pictures of the sort of house they might be living in when they reached their destination, a promise that he could choose some of his bedroom furniture and an assurance that when they came home another house would be waiting for them were sufficient to allay his fears.

Here's a poem on listening which encapsulates these skills:

When I ask you to listen to me
And you start giving advice
You have not done what I asked.
When I ask you to listen to me
And you begin to tell me why I shouldn't feel that
    way
You are trampling on my feelings.
I ask you to listen to me
And you feel you have to do something to solve my
    problems.
You have failed me, strange as that may seem.
Listen! All I asked was that you listen
Not talk or do – just hear me.

Anon

Understanding

It is very hard to be realistic about our own children – the faults and weaknesses in everyone else's children are obvious, but there is a reluctance to admit to them in our own. It is very important in a healthy family to recognise children's weakness and strengths, just as we do our own. In their weaknesses they need support and comfort; in their strengths they need encouragement and building up. Their special needs must also be registered and attended to, whether that be learning difficulties or health concerns. It is important never to be blindly defensive. It may be hard to acknowledge that one's child has special needs and parents are not guaranteed to be grateful to the person who points it out!

Whereas at school in the home country, certain learning difficulties may be uncovered in the normal course of tuition, that will not always be the case with education overseas, so it may be necessary to be particularly vigilant. For example, what are the signs of dyslexia? If testing is not part of the normal procedure, what other arrangements can be made? What forms of educational assessment can be made during a short visit home? How far in advance do arrangements have to be made?

When a child has limited language ability, they can often be regarded as 'stupid'. Parents need to be aware of the sort of difficulties their children might be encountering in a second language situation and take appropriate action. This may mean contacting the school or just providing reassurance for the child.

Other needs may be emotional and not easily rationalised. They may relate to self-esteem. A senior missionary speaks of her own experience as a child:

When I was a small girl, I tended to be rather insecure. I had a very brilliant brother who was the light of his parents' eyes because he was so good academically. I had a very popular sister and I was rather at the end of the line. One golden day, I was selected to be the silver paper fairy for a church programme. We had been collecting for a year to give to a good cause and I was to be the silver paper fairy and to stand on the platform with a wand. I was five and I was going to be in charge. Half an hour before the programme, the organisers came to me and said, 'You're not going to be the silver paper fairy. We've selected your sister instead.' I thought my heart would break. I needed to be the silver paper fairy.

Affirmation

This is often perceived as a very American concept and therefore to have no place in European families. In practice of course we do affirm our children. We like to praise them when they have done well or when they have attempted something even if they did not succeed. Hopefully, success is not considered a measure of their achievement. Shy and diffident children need reassurance and encouragement to try things that their bolder siblings don't think twice about attempting. Affirmation comes from recognising strengths and weaknesses and complimenting them accordingly.

One family I knew had two sons. John was very bright academically, Luke struggled in that area but was a good athlete and musician. John was encouraged to pursue an academic career but Luke was valued just as much by the family; the father went cross-country running with him and money was found for music lessons. Each has a very good sense of self-worth.

Part of affirmation, too, is giving children a voice in decision-making, asking their opinion, showing that they are loved and respected and share your concerns. Older children in particular should be involved in decision-making processes. Children fare much better overseas if they perceive the value of their parents' work and feel they have a share in it. This is particularly important where parents are overseas because of a sense of vocation.

Balance

'My dad works too hard – for very good reasons, but I don't like it.'

There are many children everywhere who would identify with that statement. If in a child's mind it is associated with being overseas, it can produce a negative reaction to the experience and a hostile attitude towards the environment, the local people and the current schooling.

Setting our priorities is never easy, between the external work, that done outside the family, and the internal, what goes on inside the family. Relationships take time. So often parents excuse themselves for spending little time with their families by calling it 'quality time' – there's not much of it but it's special for that reason. Such an excuse is frequently merely self-justification and self-deception.

It is hard to get the balance right. Some see only the work, some only the family. Where there is the third element of some kind of ministry to the community, it becomes a three-way struggle. It's an area that needs constant re-examination. Resolving conflicts within the family takes time – time to air grievances and resentments at the earliest possible opportunity.

It is important to discover ways of spending time together, of juggling the demands of work and home, particularly overseas where the jobs may offer large financial rewards but require working hours that are so punishing as to rule out any life outside. Some families have to face the question, 'Is it worthwhile taking the whole family overseas when the wage-earner will have so little free time?' In that case the alternatives have to be given serious consideration. How long will the separation be? What provision is there in the contract for air fares which will enable the family to get together on a regular basis? If the wage-earner has a significant role overseas, how far is it possible for him/ her to negotiate more free time? Can he/she acquire more control over the timetable?

Coping with separation

In many overseas assignments, it is necessary for the bread-winner to spend a lot of time travelling away from the family. This is hard on the whole family but particularly on the spouse staying at home. It is important for partners to discuss the pressures involved in prolonged or frequent absences and to be open about how they feel, particularly the one remaining behind, or resentments may fester. Similarly, it helps to talk to the children before departure about the nature of the assignment, the sort of people who will be there and how long the visit will be. It's helpful, too, to put up pictures of the place and talk about it with the children. Leaving behind something which will be gradually used up whilst away helps young children to know how the time passes. One parent I know leaves a pile of M&Ms, one for each day, to be consumed while he's away.

Families adopt their own special ways of keeping in touch when separated. Some husbands and wives leave a note to be found in the suitcase and under the pillow when they've gone. Apart from the obvious email and phone calls, it's a good idea to send or collect postcards of the visit. Another good idea is to keep a diary whilst away that can be shared upon return – memory is very fallible, especially when it gets very busy. Most parents bring back gifts from their trips; it doesn't have to be anything big, but make it significant. For instance, clothing from the area, things representing the five senses that can be experienced rather than just stored up, or something to add to an existing collection.

Planning, not just for the trip, but for the family is a vital activity. For the spouse remaining, it's good to plan some special events to take place during the other's absence. Then the family can hold a special celebration to mark the return. My children used to enjoy making banners or cards and we'd have a special meal or cake together. If possible, the trips should be spaced carefully for frequency and duration. Consideration should be given to whether it might be possible for an older child to accompany the parent occasionally on trips away.

Nourishing your relationship

My husband has a screen-saver on his computer which reads: 'The best thing a father can do for his children is to love their mother.' – and a pretty good job he's made of it, I have to say!

If the basis of a healthy family platform is the relationship between the parents, what can parents do to nourish that relationship? There are plenty of self-help books on marriage, but we're becoming a less literate and book-oriented society, so where else do we go for help? I would recommend one of the marriage enrichment weekends which are available. This can be a very valuable way of exploring ways of communication and of spending some time alone together when you're home after a hectic spell abroad.

Or if you'd like a short-hand approach, here are some questions you might find helpful.

1. What is your greatest obstacle to quality husband-wife together time?
2. Do you believe you have intimacy needs that are not fully met?
3. Identify one step you could take to achieve greater intimacy in any of these areas: emotional, intellectual, spiritual, recreational, physical.
4. When you were growing up, how was the expression of feelings encouraged or discouraged in your family?
5. What conditions need to be present for you to feel free to share yourself with your partner?
6. Share an area where you feel you specially need encouragement and support from your partner.

Finding time and opportunity to nourish the husband/wife relationship can be problematic in some overseas cultures and couples need to think of creative ways around social restrictions. Further consideration will be given to this in chapter eight.

The following is a suggested strategy for problem-solving within the family. The family should sit down together and agree the plan and then work together through the steps.

1. What is the problem we are having?
2. What is the end result we would like to see?
3. What are the possible ways in which we could resolve the problem?
4. What seems to be the best plan we could use?
5. Agree to implement the plan you have devised. Write down exactly what the family does to follow it.
6. Did the plan work? How do you know? Evaluate the outcome.

Family life cycle

Finally, I am indebted to Dr Kelly O'Donnell[3] for his permission to reproduce the following tripartite developmental model of the expatriate family. Three types of developmental stages are represented: the development of the family as a unit, the individual developmental stages of each family member, and the career stages of the parents.

The Family Life Cycle begins with an unattached young adult going overseas who may gain some cross-cultural experience. Next comes the newly married couple who may be bonding not just with each other but also with a new

FAMILY LIFE CYCLE

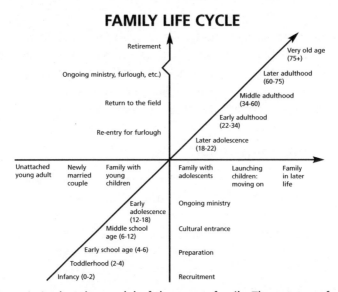

Figure 1: A tripartite model of the expat. family. Three types of developmental stages are represented: FLC, individual, and career stages.

Development Tasks of Expat. Families at Different FLC Stages

FLC	Realignment of Generations	Renegotiation of Roles
Unattached Young Adult	1. Geographic and cultural distance furthers differentiation from family. 2. Individual becomes a member of a new family – the expat. team.	1. Experimentation with adult roles and identity as an expat. 2. Choice of spouse and direction of future family influenced by missions.
Newly Married Couple	1. Boundaries for newly married affected by geographic distance from families. 2. Geographic distance limits emotional support from families of origin.	1. Assuming spousal and missionary roles simultaneously is difficult. 2. Different expectations for husband and wife roles in the host culture.
Family With Young Children	1. Need to find a "family niche" and "affiliated family" in the host culture. 2. Different boundary expectations: time together as a family and privacy issues. 3. Presence of children can create "inter-cultural links" with nationals.	1. Childbearing and childrearing may be deferred for the sake of career. 2. Different socialisation experiences: language, customs, and schooling. 3. Multiple roles and role confusion for missionary wives creates stress.
Family With Adolescents	1. Separation via boarding school: early launching and empty nest experiences. 2. Extended family relationships continue to be limited by geographic distance.	1. Peer group identification difficulty in cultural entrance and reentry stages. 2. Midlife issues for husbands and wives: identity, marriage, career.
Launching Children; Moving On	1. Grown child must choose a country and culture into which to launch. 2. Young adult may "trial launch" in the proximity of extended family members who live in the parent's homeland.	1. New nonparental roles may free the couple for more work in overseas posts. 2. Desire to contribute to future generations in middle-age may increase community involvement.
Family in Later Life	1. Desire to care for aged parents may postpone going overseas. 2. Retired expat. may seek to live close to or with family.	1. Retirement abroad as an expat. is a possibility. 2. Expat. role affected by the health of the older adult.

excerpted from O'Donnell, K., *Journal of Psychology and Theology*, 1987, Volume 15 (4); also reprinted in *Helping Missionaries Grow* (1988, William Carey Library) culture. Then follows the family with young children where new responsibilities are assumed, the family with adolescent children which is often a period of conflict, the stage where the children move on, often called the 'empty nest syndrome', and finally the stage leading to retirement.

Questions for parents

1. Examine your own upbringing. What would you like to imitate and what would you like to avoid?
2. Who takes responsibility for discipline in the family? Do you have an agreed strategy with which you both feel comfortable?
3. Write down three strengths and three weaknesses for each child. What can you do to affirm them in these areas?
4. When you sit down to discuss a situation, can you reflect back what your partner has said on the subject? How do you need to improve your listening skills?
5. Does your current lifestyle give you adequate family time, in your opinion? In what ways will the new situation be different?
6. Do you actively seek time together alone without the children? What opportunities will there be for this in the new situation?

Notes
1. *God in the Wasteland*, by David F. Wells, published by IVP, 1994.
2. 'Suffering – when does it become unethical?' by Marjory F. Foyle. Published in *Interact*, May 1992, Volume 1 (4).
3. 'Family Life Cycle' by Dr Kelly O'Donnell, published in the *Journal of Psychology and Theology*, 1987, volume 15 (4).

Chapter 3

Transition – Making Moves

'Transitions can be keenly anticipated or feared. They can be stepping stones to maturity and new stages of life or they can be fraught with uncertainty and inconclusiveness and laced with pain' – W.D. Taylor[1]

Transition can be defined as the movement of people from one stage of life to another or from one cultural context to another. In this chapter we shall be looking mainly at the latter. Families going overseas experience transition every time they leave or enter a country. Much of what will be written applies not only to TCKs but also to adults. If parents understand what is going on in transition, they can prepare their children for it and help them through it. They can also help others to understand what the family is going through so that more realistic support and assistance can be given to them whether at a distance when overseas or at first hand when returning home.

In the TCK profile it was noted that the TCK may be surrounded by, or be part of, several cultures. Firstly, there is the home culture or cultures of the parents, then the culture of the host country, which may be broken down into sub-groups, especially where parents are working in a tribal situation, the culture of the school environment which may be national, multi-national, mono-cultural but of a culture not his own, such as American schools for European children, the church culture, and the cultures of other people working alongside his parents.

Change is a normal part of life for everyone and particularly part of any transition. But the amount of stress is intensified by two things: the period of time involved – the shorter the time, the more painful the experience; and the difference between the point of departure and the point of completion.

With cross-cultural transition, there is an adjustment out of and an adjustment into a very different situation each time. Moreover, it's getting faster all the time. Martin, a TCK in his 40s, can remember the time when as a family they set sail for Libya and spent a few months getting there. It was a bit like taking a cruise. Those days are long since gone and with them the opportunity to adjust, reflect and contemplate the new situation. Within a few hours of boarding the plane one could be in a different world. Also, whilst people anticipate problems in moving to the new culture, they do not expect them in returning home.

It has already been mentioned that the way someone leaves one situation affects the way they enter the next. Unfinished business in the area of personal relationships most significantly destroys the ability to start in a new situation. In other words, troubles are not left behind, they are exported to a different environment. Dr Marjorie Foyle in her study on why Christian workers with difficulties return home, has found that in the majority of cases, the problems existed before they left home and have merely been exacerbated or given fresh scope for expression in the new location.

Unresolved situations and stress are carried over into the new situation. Moreover, the closer a person is to leaving, the less likely they are to deal with conflicts. This is just as true for children as for adults, so we all need to learn to take leave of people well. In American studies on transition, bringing a period of one's life to a satisfactory conclusion is described as making 'good closures'. In the busyness of packing up and getting ready to go, the need to set things right at work, in the neighbourhood and in the extended family is squeezed out by the shortage of time and the pressures of imminent departure. The tyranny of the urgent, as always, overrides the important.

The Transition Experience

I reproduce on p.50 the model developed by Dave Pollock called 'The Transition Experience'.[2] It helps to chart the flow of moving from one culture to another. Social Status refers to how people perceive and respond to you. Social Posture is how you respond to others and Psychological Experience describes how you feel about it.

Involvement

The first stage, Involvement, is where people are before they leave – secure in their position in society, work, the family and church or similar social organisations. It is characterised by participation, feeling part of things. Alongside that feeling goes the ability to take decisions, to operate freely and with confidence. For a child this is represented by its role in school, neighbourhood friendships, clubs and societies, and the place it holds in the extended family.

Leaving

At the second stage, Leaving, there is a peculiar mixture of celebration and grief as ties are loosened, responsibilities are relinquished and new roles anticipated.

THE TRANSITION EXPERIENCE[2]

	INVOLVEMENT	LEAVING	TRANSITION	ENTERING	RE-INVOLVEMENT
Social Status	**Belonging** Part of 'in' group Reputation Position Knowing	**Celebration** Attention Recognition Farewells Closures	**Statusless** Unknown Lack of structure Special Knowledge without use	**Introducing** Marginality Mentor searching Uncertain of position/response Misinterpretation of behaviour-signals	**Belonging** Known Knowing Position
Social Posture	**Committed** Responsible Responsive	**Distancing** Loosen Ties Relinquish roles Disengage	**Chaos** Must initiate relationships Isolation Self-centred Exaggerated problems Ambiguity/ misunderstanding	**Superficial** Observer Uncertain of trust Exaggerated behaviour Risk taking Search for mentor Errors in response	**Committed** Belonging Involved Conforming behaviour Concern for others
Psychological Experience	**Intimacy** Confirmed Secured	**Denial** Rejection Resentment Sadness Guilt Anticipation (expectations) ——→	**Anxiety** Loss of self-esteem Loss of continuity/ sacred objects Grief from loss Emotional instability Dreams Disappointment ——→ Panic	**Vulnerability** Fearful Ambivalent Easily offended Depression Psychosomatic problems	**Intimacy** Secure Affirmed
	(Present oriented)	(Future/Temporary)	(Future)	(Present/Temporary)	(Present/Permanent)

There are parties to say goodbye, and gifts are exchanged alongside tearful farewells to those with whom the family's life has been linked. The decision to take a family overseas may come in for some criticism, particularly from anxious grandparents who will also be fearful of their ability to maintain close links over long distances. This stage is often accompanied by a degree of guilt for the situation and people left behind, responsibilities that can no longer be adequately fulfilled and which consequently may fall more heavily on others' shoulders.

For children going overseas for the first time, there may be no sense of anticipation, only a sense of loss. Conversely, for those born overseas, those emotions may be felt more acutely when coming 'home' because for them the overseas location is home. They have no ties back in the 'home' country, nothing to return to.

It is generally recognised that disengagement from a situation begins six months before the actual event. At that stage comes a psychological withdrawal, a distancing from relationships, commitments and responsibilities. With people going overseas on shorter contracts, it's not hard to see that some are in perpetual transition – a most uncomfortable experience! One parent said to me, 'I live with my suitcase mentally packed.'

Transition

The third stage, Transition, marks the arrival in the new country or situation. The degree of discomfort and alienation felt will depend on the degree of difference from the home culture and the depth of involvement anticipated in the new. For those who go to live on an expatriate compound, where the object is to produce mini-England, mini-France or mini-USA and restrict contact with the national culture to the minimum, the stress may be lessened. Mentally, adults may never really leave their home culture. It is far less likely that children will retain that frame of mind. They tend to assimilate parts of the host culture without their parents being aware of it.

In Transition, the traveller becomes lost with no defining role or identity. He or she has specialist skills without the ability or opportunity to use them and limited responsibilities to exercise. The ability to communicate and function normally is impaired by inadequate understanding, language and lack of appropriate knowledge. Life is centred on surviving and minor difficulties assume major proportions. A good summing-up word is CHAOS!

The problem for a family is that at this time, parents are so focused on the need to survive and cope with their own problems that they are very often unaware of the struggles their children are having or unable to take them on board and give them due care and attention. One mother told me that on their return to the UK having lived in nine different houses in fourteen weeks, when asked by her son how to cope with a certain task she screamed 'How do you expect me to know? I can't cope with what I've got to do!' and then felt guilty for saying it.

At this stage sleep patterns may be affected and emotional and spiritual balances upset. It is important to recognise that these are the normal symptoms of transition, not the result of inadequacy or personal failure. If a child is waking up frequently or having nightmares, they may need reassurance that their world is still holding together rather than needing medication.

Entering

The fourth stage, that of Entering, describes the time when things are beginning to come together and make sense, when the situation takes on a degree of familiarity. However, there is a tendency to be tentative in what you say and do and a fear of doing the wrong thing. The new language is being tried and mistakes are inevitably made. Most families who live overseas have a rich store of 'howlers' with which to entertain their friends! However, this can be very unnerving, especially when offence is caused by the use of the wrong word or the wrong gesture. It is very easy to send out the wrong non-verbal signals. Learning the appropriate mannerisms and body language is a slow process. It can take a long time to put some of these mistakes right.

Having used the wrong hand when saying goodbye, one couple took weeks on their return to restore relationships with their neighbours. Language, on the other hand, is best learnt by those prepared to take the risks and make some mistakes. In most countries, people are appreciative of the effort being made.

Children often spend a long time watching and listening, making sure they've got it right before joining in with the peer group. Matthew and his family moved from Asia back to Scotland. His parents were concerned when their normally very talkative 10-year-old was remarked on by his teacher as having very little to say for himself. This continued for about six months at the end of which he came out in the broadest Glaswegian accent imaginable – far more accentuated than most of his class-mates!

Sometimes it is the shyer, more introverted child who makes a better start than his extrovert sibling. This is because, whilst the introvert is quietly standing by, watching and listening, the extrovert is wading in with two feet, making himself known, making mistakes and sometimes earning a reputation which it takes a while to shrug off. Parents, conversely, expect the extrovert to make it and give more support to the introvert. It pays to watch both carefully and pick up the nuances of what's going on when they may not be prepared to tell you openly how things are going.

Dr Richard Woolfson in his book *From Birth to Starting School* says: 'Go the extra yard emotionally. Check with your

Problems with integration into Scottish society.

Families on the Move

children after a couple of weeks. Ask: "How is the new bedroom, how is the new school, is there anything I can help with?" It is not a static process.'[3]

Re-engagement

At the final stage, Re-engagement, the situation is more or less back where it started. Once again, there are friends, neighbours and colleagues, people who recognise who you are and where you belong, who can 'pigeon-hole' you satisfactorily. The focus of attention moves from one's own needs to those of others and there is a sense of belonging and commitment.

It is usually at this point that someone decides it's time for you to be up and off again! Timing these moves is crucial for children. There are times in their personal life cycle and in their academic life cycle when moving is really not a good idea and should be avoided at all costs. A little forward thinking can often prevent unnecessary trauma in this area.

Whatever strategies are put in place to cope with moving the first time, need to be revived for the return trip. It is important to allow oneself and one's children to do the farewells in culturally appropriate ways. Just as there is a proper place for education about a new country before living there, so, too, children need to be educated about the country to which they are returning especially if they have never spent a significant amount of time there.

Coping with grief

The downside to the TCK experience is the sense of loss, grief and stress which all TCKs express. One TCK aged 11 wrote to me: 'I was 4 months old when I went to Ethiopia. I lived there for 7 years. I really want to go back; there's lots of crying and emotions.'

Even good changes are stressful, and in multiple

transition there is a lot of disorientation, exhaustion and grief. This may express itself in anger, withdrawal, or depression. For some there is overwhelming regret and nostalgia, but for others a bitterness for what they have been denied. It is important that TCKs are helped to handle and express these emotions rather than suppress them. Grief that is not expressed becomes suppressed but will eventually come out, even if it is some years later and may be the more traumatic because of the time that has elapsed. If the symptoms are not recognised, the child can end up feeling a victim and become angry and depressed, with a sense of no-one really caring how he or she feels.

There may not be adequate opportunities to express grief. Or there may be no-one with whom the child can grieve, no-one who understands what they are experiencing. And grieving takes time, it is a process. Losing home, friends, a cultural identity is like a bereavement, especially since it may involve a place to which they never have the chance to return. In the multitude of celebrations that take place at a time of farewells, the child may feel guilty at having negative feelings or indeed excitement may preclude grief. One TCK, again someone in her 40s, wrote: 'It wasn't until returning to Kenya many years later that I realised how much "home" it had been. I still have a longing to return.'

The RAFT strategy

In addition to the Transition Experience, Dave Pollock has produced a very helpful formula for enabling people to say goodbye and with his permission I reproduce it here. It's called the RAFT strategy.

R – Reconciliation
A – Affirmation
F – Farewells
T – Think Destination

Reconciliation

Reconciliation means rebuilding relationships, forgiving and being forgiven, making your peace with those you're leaving behind. Jesus talks about the two sides of this in Matthew and Luke's Gospels. In Matthew, he says, 'If your brother has something against you, be reconciled to your brother' (Matthew 5:23–24), and in Luke he says, 'If you have something against your brother forgive him' (Luke 17:3). Someone has to take the initiative in effecting reconciliation, and parents can model this for children in their own relationships.

Affirmation

Affirmation means expressing appreciation for the past, even if it wasn't all good. It prevents a separation from becoming a funeral. Children may have had negative experiences but they can learn from them. If as adults we affirm our negative experiences, it helps children to reflect positively on theirs. Parents who constantly criticise their situation or the country in which they live make it very difficult for their children to settle.

Farewells

Farewells means saying goodbye properly to people, places and pets, in culturally appropriate ways. In some countries this means the celebrations go on for some days and involve considerable hospitality. If goodbyes are not said properly, there is a sense of incompleteness. One TCK spoke of being picked up from her school and being whisked off to the airport without having the chance to say goodbye to the lady who looked after her, the cat or the next-door neighbours.

It is particularly hard on those who have been subjected to crisis repatriation, where the speed of evacuation left no time to make any preparation, disposition of possessions or opportunity to say goodbye to special people. For some this remains a long-term grief as there is no opportunity to return to the country for either political or financial reasons.

Anne was sitting in on a session where I was speaking about this subject. I gradually became aware that rather than observing she was sitting there with tears streaming down her cheeks. Some eight years previously her family had been evacuated in a medical emergency and they had never had the opportunity to return – and it still caused her pain.

Think Destination

Think Destination is a stimulus to be realistic about what awaits the family at the other end of leaving. Many parents return home wearing rose-coloured spectacles. They have fond memories of how life was before they left the old country and impart these dreams to their children. For many there comes a rude awakening. Much has changed during their absence and memory has a funny way of glossing over and erasing the unpleasant aspects of our past. If a degree of reality is not present, disillusionment can easily set in and adjustment is made all the harder.

There is a practical side to Thinking Destination. What plans have been made for housing? How much have banking systems changed? Will there be adequate funds in the home bank account to cover the costs of resettlement? Is it necessary to enter children into the desired school before leaving? Certainly some plans regarding their future education should be made before leaving the current school. What help will be available upon return and who will be there to offer it? Further discussion of these issues is to be found in chapter eight on Re-Entry.

Communication is going to be a key to coping with transition – both the way we communicate with home and the way we communicate with our children – the degree of honesty we display, the ability to convey feeling as well as fact, acknowledging the differences we discover without implying criticism. Maintaining the links and sustaining that communication is the subject of a later chapter. The quote with which this chapter begins ends in this way: 'The key is the family culture and the agency support system which by a pastoral counselling policy strengthens family units.' There is an onus on companies and sending agencies to support the family through transition in any way they can.

Many TCKs find it hard to articulate how they feel about their experiences of moving and many find a release in creative writing or drawing. The following is a poem by a TCK who was born in Egypt, and subsequently spent time in Jordan, France and Cyprus.

Droplets
a reflection on moving

Once upon a time, there was a storm brewing in the sky and rain droplets were getting ready to drop. All the droplets were scared so they were all reassuring each other it was time to go.

They screamed with terror as they free fell but they soon began to enjoy it. Soon enough the ground neared towards them and their potential resting place was clear to them.

The droplets fell in different areas. Some were happy and some were not. The happy ones fell on their fellow rivers and lakes but the unhappy ones fell on sewage dumps and into drains.

But one day all those droplets from the storm disappeared from their resting places and re-emerged, once again in the clouds. As they met up with friends, all the droplets had experiences to tell.

Katie Fraser-Smith, aged 17

Questions

1. Where would you identify yourself as being in the Transition Experience?
2. Have you ever been through this before? Can you identify the feelings you had at the time?
3. How do you cope with change? Think of one major change in your life and how you dealt with it.
4. Do you or anyone in your family have 'unfinished business' which needs to be resolved before you leave?
5. Where do you expect to find mentors for yourself and your children in the new situation?
6. How do you feel about initiating relationships? Are your children good at making friends? What help can you give them?

Notes

1. 'A TCP String of Five Pearls', by William D. Taylor, published in *Interact*, December 1994.
2. 'Transition Model' taken from *The Third Culture Kid Experience*, by Dave Pollock and Ruth van Reken and reproduced with permission.
3. *From Birth to Starting School*, by Dr Richard Woolfson, published by Caring Books.

MOVED OR MOVING?

HERE ARE SOME "TIPS"
TO PREVENT THE "PITS"

That's where you start...
... from the bottom!

NOTE ONE please read this page from the foundations up.
NOTE TWO some may not make much sense now but when you leave, you'll need to be able to hang your memories on some facts.

CHANGE

A bend in the road is not the end of the road, unless you fail to make the turn

Make your own way: don't depend on your brother or sister. (14–17)		Get to know the history of the country as well as the religion. I regret I didn't. (18+)
Don't expect the new place to be like the last or like heaven! (11–17)	Find someone older and wiser to talk to about being a teenager, to act like a counsellor. (18+)	
The grass may seem greener where you came from. *(ED. So water the ground under your feet.)* (18+)	Enjoy friendships with the local population. (14–17).	Don't rebel against your surroundings (18+)
Find a school mate to whom you can safely put all your dumb questions. (18+)	You're not alone. There are lots of kids like us who move, who come from somewhere else! (14–17)	
Learn what is 'normal', check it against your faith, then fit in. (18+)		Be on your guard. They'll try to trick you. (11–13)
Be ready to meet and make new friends – of all nationalities. Don't be afraid. (11–18+)	If you really do hate the place, make the effort to like it because in the end you will discover it was worth it. (18+)	
Make good friends of your own type (not just the most friendly), and at your own speed. (11–18+)		Learn the new language as fast as possible. (11–13)
Expect to adapt: children are good at that. (18+)	Think positively. Pretend you are on a great adventure. (11–13)	Have fun. Enjoy yourself. (11–17) Don't let yourself feel discouraged. (11–13)
Buy a memory. (ed) PRAY	Gets lots of addresses and keep in touch. (14–17)	Say goodbye to the last place properly, as if you may never return. It's really hard. (11–17)
Talk the move through thoroughly with your parents before you move Say what you really think. (18+)	Take lots of photos of where you have recently lived. (18+)	Find out about the place before you go, the politics... (11–13)

▶ Chapter 4

Preparing to Go

Most people these days will move house,
change job, relocate, at some point in their
lives. We live in a highly mobile society. An
English national newspaper recently produced two articles
about the experience of families moving from one part of
the United Kingdom to another. Under the heading 'Moving
house: is it always a nightmare for children?' comes the
subheading: 'For adults, moving house is a stressful
experience. But for children, it can be even more traumatic.'

When they move, most people take the opportunity to
visit the area, see the schools, decide what sort of area they
want to live in, investigate the public transport and settle
when they find a location that feels like a good fit.

When you're moving several thousand miles away, you
don't have that luxury. But that doesn't mean you have to
trust to chance and go out blindfolded. There is much that
can be done to prepare both your child and yourself to face
the move and cope better with the transition. The advent of
video and internet information makes it possible to visit
places and get information that is both visual and
interactive, unlike simple travel books.

Agencies and firms that are sending out families need

to realise that they too have a responsibility and role in giving adequate time and preparation to those families both before they leave and during their time overseas. When the support networks that were present in the home country are removed, the organisation responsible for their welfare needs to know what is available to replace those supports and what else may need to be put in place.

A number of charities have subscribed to the document 'People in Aid', a code of best practice for those working with aid agencies. It ensures that those in the relief sector are well treated as personnel. Most firms will have their own codes of best practice in the area of human resources. I would like to suggest that in the case of those sending whole families overseas, this should be extended to a commitment to exercise care over the whole family, both before, during and after the assignment.

Selection

Good preparation and care of the family going overseas starts at the selection procedure. As well as the interviews for job competence, the family should be given an opportunity to voice concerns and to work through the issues confronting them. Their ability to cope with such transitions and the resources they have acquired should be assessed.

Several Christian agencies use the services of 'Interhealth' to enable their members to have a psychological screening, not necessarily to determine acceptance or rejection but to help in the direction of applicants. Interhealth is a Christian agency based in London offering medical and psychological screening to those going overseas, ongoing medical care between assignments and debriefing services upon return, for individuals and families.

I have already said that families with adolescent

children should not go overseas for the first time. Adolescents are going through enough life changes without the added stress of cultural transition. Parents with children of any age who are unwilling to go should also be discouraged as should those with major unresolved issues in their lives. These are cases where saying 'no' to an assignment is a matter of caring for those concerned. Sometimes a conflict of interests is denied because of fear, fear of losing one's job or fear of losing face because of seeming inadequate to the task.

Agencies and companies need to address the issue of involving children in the selection process. Is there any way they have a voice, even if only to express fears and misgivings, some of which will be easily allayed? Is there anyone who can take on a personnel function for children?

Orientation

Orientation needs to take place for the whole family, not just the parents with baby-sitting facilities provided for the children. A further look at the issues raised in chapter two will suggest ways forward in this area. It is helpful if personnel departments are aware of differences between the generations – the boosters, boomers, and busters, as they are sometimes called – and their attitude to work and family. The welfare of children is an important factor in determining the probable success of an overseas assignment. If good care systems are put in place for the whole family, they are likely to remain in place for a longer time and to function more effectively.

Companies should also have the resources to provide good orientation on the country, people, customs and language of the host country. This should involve not just the etiquette of what to do when you are invited to the embassy function, but social manners, how to greet people, offer hospitality, go visiting, make payments, comply with legal requirements. Where organisations are consistently sending out large numbers of families, it is easy to build up a store of resources and to put on a regular orientation course. When it is just an individual family unit involved, this can get overlooked. In spite of mass-marketing and mass-production, there is still a need to emphasise the importance and worth of the individual.

Many firms now put on a basic introduction to the language before families leave for the field. Unfortunately this is often just for the wage-earner rather than for the whole family. If the husband is the employee, the wife is more likely to need language in order to be able to function at the level of neighbourhood society, such as doing basic shopping, taking the children to the doctor and dealing with local services.

Preparation for parents

Reading the first three chapters of this book is a good place to start! Once we understand the nature of the TCK profile and the mechanics of transition, it is easier to plan and take steps to limit the stress and anxiety entailed. The insecurity of living in a foreign culture often makes parents over-anxious, whereas seeing the flow of transition, and recognising the normal reactions to it, lessens the anxiety. It is very important to discern the stresses associated with growing up in an unfamiliar culture and separate them from the normal stresses of family life. All children go through the 'terrible twos' and the trials of adolescence. Knowing what is usual in those stages helps parents not to become paranoid about their situation.

And that's the second step to take. Parents should be sure to arm themselves with a good book on normal childhood development, something that spells out the characteristics of the preschool child, a child in the early-school years and so on. It is useful to have guidelines on physical, social and emotional development and the age by which certain skills should have been acquired.

Although many expatriate situations provide the same facilities as home, in an isolated situation overseas it may be very difficult to find a norm or standard by which you can gauge your child's development. Expectations differ in other cultures. It is a mistake to judge one child's development by what a previous child achieved. A map of some sort is very helpful. The appendix includes a brief summary of childhood development by Dr Marjory F. Foyle as a starting point (see p. 175).

The question should be asked, who is on site already and knows the ropes? If you can find another family already in the location, write to them about the things that matter to you. The following questions might be included. What sort of schools are there? If you have to find your own housing, which neighbourhood would they advise you to live in, given your priorities (e.g. distance from schools, work, shops, transport)? How about food and diet? Is there anything you should bring especially that can't be obtained there and that your family can't do without? For the majority of Brits I know, it's a large jar of marmite!

Another area that features high on most parents' agendas is health concerns. I am assuming that families are informed prior to departure of the injections they need before they leave and of any preventative treatments they can have. But what opportunity is there to receive boosters, if required, once you are overseas? Some countries now require regular AIDS testing, to prove freedom from infection. Are the needles used for such tests safe?

Further, are there any particular health risks associated with that part of the world? What sort of overall health care is available to you on location? Is it necessary to take any special medication with you because it is unlikely to be available on site? Does the company or agency have a policy on emergency treatment? Are there certain conditions which should be considered untreatable in your location and for which you should have contingency plans to evacuate? Who is responsible for health insurance?

Interhealth produce an excellent booklet called 'Good Health, Good Travel', described as a guide for backpackers, travellers, volunteers and overseas workers. They also produce two health update letters a year on current concerns and risks. Reading the book will minimise avoidable sickness overseas. It is also good to be armed with a home medical book on childhood diseases.

If at all possible, parents should get a good grounding in the cultural norms and expectations of the country to which they are going. If the family can measure up to the behavioural norms of the society around them, providing that does not clash with their own values and standards, then that is a major step forward in being accepted by the national community.

A child can quickly be taught the appropriate ways of greeting someone, addressing an adult, and taking the first steps in making friends. But you need to know it first!

Preparation for children

I have already stressed the importance of communication with children and good communication can assuage a lot of the fears and uncertainty children feel before entering a new situation. I have produced a handbook which I use with TCKs to help prepare them for life overseas. Through games, artwork, creative writing, pictures and questions, it looks at their family identity and ways of preserving that as well as tackling some of the differences they are going to encounter.

For children, much of their sense of security comes from the domestic stability surrounding where they live. Uprooting and moving thousands of miles away means removing that stability. Talking about the move well in advance, stressing the positive benefits of the move and discussing the options open to them, helps smooth the way for children making the change.

Children who are quite young can take in and process an amazing amount of information. Ellie and her family were going to Indonesia. Ellie was just 5. I sat over a meal table and Ellie told me all about the houses in Indonesia, how they were on stilts and why that was necessary. She could tell me the sort of food she would be eating and, yes, mummy had already cooked her that sort of food and she was getting to like it. She knew what school was going to be like and that mummy and daddy were going to have to learn a new language and she was going to help her small brother make new friends.

Ellie's parents had done a marvellous job of preparing her for the move. She had seen pictures and videos, she'd tasted the tastes and had a real sense of anticipation of what she was going to. She was excited at the prospect. However, parents do need to be careful of over-icing the cake, in case they raise the level of expectation too high and set the family up for a big disappointment.

It is important that children have around them things which give them a sense of continuity and Ellie had worked out precisely which toys and things precious to her that she needed to take with her. When luggage space is short, it is vital to make room for that favourite teddy bear, however tatty he may be. We all need our 'sacred object' whether it be a picture, rugs, ornaments or playthings. Having something to hang up which reminds you of 'home' gives a sense of domestic stability. One family had a particular picture, a clock and a rug that graced their sitting room wherever they were – it gave a sense of continuity amid all the impermanence.

Everyone is scared of losing things in the move. It is a good idea to let children pack some of their things well ahead of time, in boxes well labelled with their names so that they feel reassured that nothing will get left behind. Also, having not played with them for several weeks means new joy and wonder when they are unpacked. Our home was in storage for three months once and we just kept out a few things. When the move was finally completed, old treasures were rediscovered with whoops of glee and it was like having Christmas all over again!

Build a memory bank

When it comes to packing, it's also important to leave behind a well labelled box of treasures, both to enjoy afresh when you come home for holiday and also to be part of the child's memory bank. One of the pieces of advice given by TCKs was to 'Get a memory!'

Before going it's good to begin keeping a record of the significant things in a child's life – they will be thankful for it later on when they are trying to peg down their roots. Start with a scrap-book of photos, of the place where they were born, of the house they've left, the neighbours, the school, the class year photo. Then collect souvenirs, any certificates for swimming achievements or football tournaments, the programme of the nativity play, newspaper clippings related to the neighbourhood or things they were involved in. Take note of the significant people and places in your child's life and register them in some way.

A major loss mentioned by all TCKs is that of the extended family. They miss not having grandparents, aunts, uncles and cousins around. So take lots of photos of the extended family and update them regularly. Most families

'The child should take something to remind him of home.'

have access to videos and a film taken of the family together, played and enjoyed together often, lessens the feeling of distance and loss.

Anything that reminds a child of something precious can go in the memory bank. It may be some of the cards or letters received on departure. Take a few favourite childhood books, ones that were special to your child when small or that were special to you and which you want your child to love too.

Build up your resources

Assuming that parents have acquired the medical books and the books on child development, what else can they gather to resource their stay? People often want to know what they can give to a family going overseas. A request for subscriptions to magazines that deal with parenting or education is a good idea. I recommend that parents get catalogues from places like the Early Learning Centres, leaflets from the Department for Education in the UK (or its national equivalent elsewhere) on current requirements in the national curriculum and put their names on the mailing lists to ensure that they are kept up to date. With the growth of internet knowledge, it's helpful to have a list of web sites that will offer information on child-related topics. You may want to take books on food and nutrition. When writing to a family already on site, ask them what they wish they had brought.

It can often be difficult to find ways of keeping fit in an overseas environment. There is not necessarily easy access to the facilities that may have been enjoyed at home. Exercise videos abound for the adult, but what about the children? What sports will they be able to practise? Is there any equipment that can fit into a suitcase, even if it is only table tennis bats or a swingball? Adequate rest and relaxation is an important ingredient in survival and good health. What does the family enjoy doing together as relaxation? Take a few favourite board games and videos to have fun with as a family.

Simulation

As learners we retain:

- 10% of what we read
- 20% of what we hear
- 30% of what we see
- 50% of what we see *and* hear
- 70% of what we ourselves say
- 90% of what we ourselves do

In today's environment, learning is increasingly interactive, for both adults and children. Corporate videos encourage executives to role-play situations. This is seen as a better means of being equipped to deal with difficult situations. Children, too, enjoy role-playing. The faculty of imagination is very alive in children and 'pretending' comes naturally to them. If there is plenty of advance warning of an impending overseas assignment, then to create some learning situations where children can role-play their way through some of what lies ahead will help them to handle the real thing when it comes.

The meal experience

Have the children prepare a room and table for a meal 'national style'. Does this mean sitting on the floor round the table? Are there any sort of rituals to be observed prior to eating, such as hand-washing? What sort of eating implements does it involve? Serve the sort of food you can expect to be given in the new country.

The market experience

How do you 'do shopping'? If possible, have some local currency for the children to handle and set up some market stalls. How do you greet a trader? This is an opportunity for some basic language acquisition as part of the game. The children can be introduced to the idea of bartering, if this is to be part of their new culture. This can be a lot of fun if it is made as noisy as possible. Work out with children how much they should expect to pay for things – the scale of costs may be very different from what they are used to.

The health experience

It is important to help children to take care of their own health. When you have been to the market and bought some fruit, wash it together. Why does fruit need to be washed? What might happen to us if we eat the fruit without washing it? Have a day when you take a siesta. Why is that important and what is the rest of the day like, before and after it?

Go for a long walk. What do you take with you? Why is it important to wear shoes? Pack up a rucksack. Pretend it is very hot where you are walking. Why is it important to drink a lot? Can you drink the water in the stream that you've passed? If not, why not? Children might enjoy designing a health poster to illustrate one of these things which you can then display in the kitchen.

The transport experience

Pretend you are waiting for a local bus. Which side of the road does the traffic drive on? What is the bus like? Do people queue? How do you pay? Has it got seats? What's it like riding in this bus? What are the roads like? Simulating a bumpy bus ride on an unmade-up road in the dining room can cause uproar in the average suburban home but it's a lot of fun!

Jeremy was determined to try out his new bargaining skills.

Reading

There are now books which deal with the experience of moving from a biographical or fictional standpoint. It is good to read through a couple of these with your child. Not only does it prepare them for the future, they may be able to express some of their fears through identifying with the characters in the book and may feel less alone in the experience, because here is someone else who has done it. A list of suggested books is printed in the appendix.

In studies on missionary attrition it has been shown that in many instances this could have been prevented or corrected with more adequate and appropriate pre-field training. Thorough personal preparation, understanding the issues involved, realistic expectations, cultural awareness, training in appropriate skills and competences all combine to produce the ability to function well in a new environment and to counteract the problems that may be encountered.

Agencies and companies, too, need a greater awareness of family needs, knowledge of the overseas environment and a readiness to invest in training and ongoing personal support. It is important to remember that people facing transition often do not 'hear' what is being said, nor, without the experience of being there and doing it, can they recognise what is important or what questions they should be asking.

I spent a considerable time with Robert preparing him for his overseas assignment. We went through the electricity system, the best way to set up bank accounts, how to send luggage, what to expect as standard in housing, what would be useful equipment to take, what would be expensive to buy and what would be easily obtainable. About three months into his assignment I received a long letter from him which started 'I think there are several things you should know which would be useful to pass on to people coming here for the first time'. He then proceeded to make a list of most of the things I'd spoken to him about but which he hadn't bothered to note down because he thought he either knew it, or didn't need to know it.

Which all goes to prove the old adage, it's not what you say, it's what people hear that counts.

Questions

1. What strategies does your company or agency have in place to prepare workers for overseas assignments?
2. What help does it offer specifically to families and children in particular?
3. Looking ahead, what do you perceive to be the three chief areas in which you will struggle to settle?
4. Whom can you turn to for advice and support?
5. Whom can your child talk to freely about their concerns, apart from yourself?
6. What professional help will you be receiving – medical, social, vocational etc?

▶ Chapter 5

Building Bridges

L iving overseas can sometimes seem like being on another planet. Not only is the climate different – you can get to like temperatures permanently over 25 degrees (unless, like my son, you end up in Russia with temperatures at 15 below and colder!) – but the food is different, the language, the clothes, the music, the sense of humour and so on. For everyone, changing cultures means the removal of comfort zones and with them the sense of security. In this chapter we shall be looking at ways of providing continuity for children between the two cultures to which they belong so that they take their sense of security with them no matter what their geographical location.

As part of the research for this book I conducted a survey of TCKs from Africa, Asia, the Far East, Europe and the Arab world. They unanimously endorsed the experience – 'I count it a real privilege', 'I wouldn't change anything', 'An invaluable experience which I am lucky to have enjoyed' – and focused on what they felt they had gained. Most frequently mentioned were cultural awareness, friendships all over the world, language ability, independence, confidence and the climate!

Their most negative responses were reserved for coming 'home', whether for a short or long time; words such as 'alien', 'different' and 'misfit' frequently appeared. One wrote: 'Living overseas was normal for me – returning was the hard part!'

The main thing they felt they missed out on, apart from TV, sports and pop music (none of which seemed to bother them too much) was the 'English thing' (or 'American' or 'Dutch'). By that they meant a link with heritage and history, a sense of belonging. It was this sense of confusion relating to a place of belonging which was the downside of the generally appreciated 'global perspective' on life. When asked to identify 'home' most answered: 'Wherever I live', 'Wherever those I love live' or 'Don't know'.

The most positive aspect for most of those returning home was the opportunity to get to know the extended family.

We've noted how Third Culture Kids adopt the values of their host countries. Europe has predominantly political values, so children raised in Europe tend to look at life from a political viewpoint. In South America people are most important and TCKs from there tend to be very people-orientated. In Africa the land is crucial so a strong sense of the environment and protecting the land dominates. In Asia it's smells and tastes which produce a great interest in food and fragrances. In Japan and the Far East the tone of culture is that of saving face which affects the way in which relationships are developed, both personally and within society.

TCKs not only appreciate all these things, they become part of their make-up and it's very hard to identify with the aspects of home culture unless as a family you work at it. John says: 'I never felt I fitted 100% in any place except school. In India I didn't feel Indian and in Britain I didn't feel British.'

TCKs assume many of the norms of their adopted country. Their mannerisms, figures of speech, ideas of social convention reflect the society in which they have been brought up. Elizabeth said, 'I did not like my parents' country at all and last time we were there I fervently hoped I'd never have to go back again.' Strong words!

Most families who go overseas do want to spare their children the sense of being 'odd man out' and to feel a sense of belonging, of heritage, of continuity. There is a sense of pride in the culture from which they have come and a desire that their children have an affinity with it as well. The only exceptions tend to be couples in cross-cultural marriages who have not worked out for themselves where 'home' ultimately is. Because this usually means one parent letting go of his or her culture and roots, it is a very painful decision to make. Parents have to work out for themselves how to build that cultural bridge across the physical and social divide and whose help to enlist in that task. The extended family and close friends back home can ease the situation if they are informed and their active participation is sought.

Here are some suggestions of ways in which to start bridge-building. As parents talk with other families who have been through the experience they will find other ways, perhaps ones which are particularly appropriate to their own home country and situation.

Family rituals and routines

One thing above all else TCKs are seeking is continuity between the old life and the new, whether that be moving from home to host country or vice-versa. For that reason identifying certain family rituals and routines which will transcend the differences and be capable of being carried over from one culture to another is especially important. For the Maartens family it meant that Friday night was always pizza and video night wherever they were, be it Africa, Holland, UK. They always made pizza on Friday night and watched a video. In most locations now, having a video is not a luxury and if families pool their resources, you can build up quite a library. It's also a very portable gift for visiting friends to bring.

For the Wilson family the ritual was pancake night and one of the biggest disappointments in their emergency departure from the field was the fact that they left the pancake recipe behind and spent several months getting it just right again!

National festivals

As well as personal rituals, there are special national occasions in the calendar to be marked. The Brits always celebrate Christmas with turkey even in temperatures of 100°, the Scots celebrate hogmanay and Burns night, with or without haggis, the Dutch celebrate the feast of Saint Nicholas and the Americans Thanksgiving. These are important points of contact for children with their cultural heritage. The very fact that they come round at the same time every year gives some shape to family life. It may not be possible to reproduce the occasion exactly but with some creative artwork and a good imagination a fair approximation can be made.

Because people back home are celebrating the same feast at the same time, it's an opportunity to exchange greetings, cards and gifts and children can be made to feel part of the wider celebration. Making your own decorations and flags can all add to the excitement and sense of 'belonging'. The involvement of grandparents at these times helps to reassure them that they are not losing touch.

These occasions sometimes produce an opportunity to

Rediscovering the pancake recipe was not so easy as it seemed.

teach a little national history, which is very important if your child is attending a school which is not following the home country's curriculum. In many international schools it is possible to come away with little or no knowledge of European history but be able to name all 50 states of America and every American president!

Establish a link family

No child wants to appear the odd one out in a group of its peers. School uniform may have been abolished in many schools, but every child knows what are the right clothes to be seen in, the right footwear with the appropriate logo. For this reason it is crucial to keep abreast of trends, fashions, books, films, and sports whilst overseas.

Children always appreciate treats from home, though they can present dilemmas. One said:

> We were only allowed one jar of jam/marmalade etc. per month with our breakfasts. This led to a difficult dilemma – do I choose marmalade or peanut butter? Solution: share your jar of British marmalade with an American family's jar of peanut butter. We tried blending the two in one pot – I haven't tried it since!

Sending treats through the post isn't always successful either:

> My mum used to mail me a tablet of fudge but after transit it always ended up as a pile of sugar crumbs which would then be slowly sucked out of a corner of the packet – with 250g of fudge inside it could last a month!

Of course, if you can't get the real thing, you can always improvise:

One treat was to blend a spoon of instant coffee with a couple of spoons of sugar and a dash of water in a mug. Then, with the butt end of your toothbrush, 'froth' it for several hours (going about your chores in the intervals). Gradually a sugary brown foam emerges and fills the whole mug. This can then be joyously consumed as an exotic-looking Italian dessert!

On the more practical side, parents should endeavour to keep up to speed with educational changes and demands in the home country, particularly if they envisage either taking or sending their children home to complete their education.

The best way to do this is to establish a 'link family', that is, a family with children of similar ages to one's own who will undertake to write, send magazines and generally keep in touch with the national scene for children their age. If the ages of the children are widespread, it may be necessary to make two links. It is worth finding out which magazines or periodicals can be downloaded from the internet. The parent of the link family will also be able, hopefully, to keep parents informed on curriculum changes and educational expectations.

This can be very tricky, as I know to my cost. At one time, Britain seemed to be revising its national curriculum at least once a year and as fast as I sent out notice of changes, the goal-posts were moved again. By the time I tried to mix in the special exemptions for Scotland and the implications of educational choice in Europe, the situation was hopeless. The situation has improved since most educational departments now have web sites which can be consulted and contain the most up-to-date information. Most universities and colleges also have their own web sites and sometimes applications to enter can be made on the internet.

Develop a cultural autobiography

This is something that begins with what was put in the 'memory bank' prior to departure. Because TCKs do not have roots in places, they need to nourish or water the roots they do have. Memories are an important part of that nourishment.

As well as taking with them overseas photos of the place they have left, children should be encouraged to continue collecting pictures of the place in which they live now, current friends and class-mates (remember, no-one knows how long they'll be around), and holidays – these are often taken in exotic places friends at home have never dreamed of visiting and which may be too expensive ever to visit again in adulthood! Loose-leaf photo albums make this a fun activity and producing nice captions and computer graphics to go with them makes them into something special.

Compiling a family tree, with photos where possible, helps TCKs to define their place in the extended family. It also provides a good subject for correspondence in letters home and for conversation when the extended family next meets up. The photos that came out with you need to be updated – encourage friends and relatives to send photos regularly and return the favour so that you'll all know how much you've changed, not just the children.

Encourage visits from home

There's nothing like a visit from a fellow-countryman or woman to restore the flavour of the old country. Moreover, a personal visit from someone who is in contact with your support network back home, whether that be the family, the church, or the social group to which you belong, establishes a link with that group. Someone who has actually been there understands much better what it's like for the whole family. They may actually be better at conveying a realistic impression to those back home because they see the situation more objectively than those who live there all the time. It's also great to have someone who, when you return, can identify with some of the places and people with whom you work.

Even a short stay can impart a feeling of belonging. There is an immediate point of contact, conversations start with 'Do you remember that cafe?' or 'Do you remember when… ?' This particularly helps children to feel less of a stranger when they return home. I encourage churches or families to club together to send just one of their number to visit someone working overseas if no one individual can afford it. It's a really worthwhile investment when it comes to empathising, supporting and praying realistically for the family concerned.

Plan for the next visit home

Families should ask themselves the following questions, well in advance of their return:

- What is it really going to be like?
- What can we do to minimise the stress?
- Where are we going to live?
- What can we practically do in the time available?
- What does my child need to know in order to cope with the experience and make it an enjoyable time rather than a penance?

Most TCKs I know can't wait to get back to what is 'home' for them.

Is the planned visit to be during school time, in which case, are the children going to attend school? If so, where and is it necessary to reserve a place for them? What are the important elements to build into this time, for example, holiday, vocational training, time with the extended family, educational assessment, spiritual refreshment? Is anyone at the home end going to help you with that planning, find out what's available and book you in where appropriate?

What about summer camps for the children? Children can benefit enormously from spending time away from their parents with their peers, especially if they have been in a very intensive relationship with their parents because of living in an isolated situation. Some camps offer the sort of sports which are not available overseas and the opportunity to be with 'ordinary' children. Some camps make a special point of attracting TCKs. I overheard Rachel talking to a fellow TCK one summer about the camp she'd just been on. Many other TCKs had been there. 'It was wonderful,' she said, 'You didn't have to explain yourself to anyone – they knew what you were talking about.'

Sacred objects

I've already referred to these in the context of transitions, but let me repeat it here. Each of us has our 'sacred objects', things which are important to us for no necessarily logical reason but which remind us of who we are and where we belong. In some way they give us significance. When people have lost many of the things which do give them meaning, it is vital to retain the little things which help meet that loss.

Here's a list of 'losses' TCKs have compiled:

- Houses and buildings
- Parents/relatives
- Friends
- Culture/country
- Sports/teams
- Music
- Food
- Toys

- Pets
- Language
- Traditions
- Community
- Climate

For a child, it's good to have the football scarf of a favourite team to drape across the bedroom or the team poster to put on the wall, to have somewhere to display the shell collection made last summer, to keep the collar the dog wore or the star from last year's Christmas tree. Don't despise the little things.

Where there is a lot of *instability*, it really helps to provide a good sense of *continuity*. The rainbow is a good image of a bridge. It joins heaven and earth and comes at the end of or even during the rain. The bridge we build between past, present and future will prove that something beautiful can come out of even the tough times.

Questions

1. Identify the family rituals which are already present in your family. Are there ways of reinforcing them?
2. What are the most significant national traditions/interests which you need to retain in your children's lives? Do you need to take things with you in order to perpetuate them?
3. To whom do you feel close as a family? Set aside time to speak with this family, explain your needs and ask whether they are willing to support you and co-operate in this way.
4. Whom do your children know that will keep them up to date with the national

scene whilst overseas? What magazines would they like to receive?

5. In what activities do you and your children currently participate? Will these be able to continue overseas? If not, is there another activity you can start to develop now which will transfer?

6. What links do you have with educators in your home country? Have you access to resources to which you can turn? Can you find the means of compiling such a list?

Chapter 6

Educational Options

For many families who go overseas, concern for their children's education is paramount. They do not even stop to consider the other effects the experience may have on them. For this reason, I have purposely not addressed educational concerns until now. They form just one part of a much broader picture, and decision-making in this area needs to be weighed against all the other factors we have considered in the TCK experience.

Before getting down to the nitty-gritty of deciding which school, where and for how long, there are several basic issues to consider and questions which parents must ask themselves. The most fundamental of these is what is most important to you about education? We each of us have our own set of values and what comes at the top of my priority list may well not come at the top of yours. Each family has to decide for itself where its priorities lie. There is no right or wrong in this, merely a matter of preference. It does require agreement between partners on the subject and a clear concept prevents undue influence being exerted by colleagues, employers or extended family.

So step one is for parents to sit down and brainstorm on a piece of paper what they value most in education and then list those values in order of priority. For some it will be academic excellence, for others opportunities for creative work, for others the social dimension, and for others the degree of interaction with local culture. Once you have made that decision, here are some other factors to be taken into account.

Factors to consider

Long-term implications

Never take the short-term view when it comes to education. Decisions taken quite early on can determine the range of options open to your child in later life. It is important to decide what your long-term plans are. Do you foresee this child being able to return to the home country in the long-term to complete his or her education? Will the course you are considering facilitate that?

How much does this choice affect our lifestyle decisions both now and in the future? What sort of society will the child be mixing with, what expectations will develop, can we commit to continuing this style of education?

Community concerns

It is assumed that parents have discussed and decided upon the degree of involvement the family will have in local culture and community. How far does the decision you are making foster or hinder that development? What are the social effects on your child? How will the decision be perceived by those with whom you are in community?

Financial implications

What is the cost of the total package? How do you foresee this being funded? What will happen if you move to a new location or if your job changes? How big will the discrepancy be between what you can afford now and what you could afford if you returned home?

Academic credibility

We will look at this in depth later on, but initially parents have to decide by what standard they are going to measure a school's academic credibility. What is to be the yardstick? What is the quality of the teaching staff? What facilities are there available for study, library, laboratories, computers, sports? How compatible is it with the home system? Does the home country recognise the qualifications on offer?

Focus of attention

Because many parents feel insecurity arising out of living in a foreign culture, undue emphasis can be laid on education and parents can become over-anxious. If they are not careful, the education of their children becomes ego-supportive. By that I mean that we judge our success or failure as parents by the comparative success or failure of our children academically.

In no way should our children be made to bear the brunt of being the yardstick by which we measure our success, either academically or personally. A parent can only do his or her best for the child. Ultimately a child grows up, makes its own way and its own decisions. We can make that easier or harder for them, but we cannot be judged by their success or failure.

Moves

When considering what is best for children in the sphere of education, parents must recognise that sometimes their assignments and moves will be affected if not dictated by their children's educational needs. We have already said that children tend to be very resilient but one move can be a move too many. There are certain points in a child's academic career when it is foolhardy to move him or her. Families must think well in advance about the timing of their moves and if some disruption is inevitable, consider how this can be minimised. Occasionally there is the possibility of leaving a child with another family known to you for a short period in order to see the child over a difficult transition and allow it to progress.

Above all, parents, whatever their priorities, need to realise that education is not just academic, it is about the whole person. In evaluating the options open to them, they need to consider the needs of the whole child, of the individual child and weigh them against the broader picture.

Types of schools

Here is an outline of most of the options available to families overseas.

National/Local schools

These may be in the national language, or in the language of the original colonising power, e.g. French schools in North Africa, British schools in parts of India, Dutch schools in Surinam. The curriculum may or may not be Western and the teaching methods may be very different, for example rote learning.

International day schools

These are usually American with multi-national staff and are to be found in large cities. They are run on a profit basis and pay Western salaries so the fees are usually high. They serve not only the international expatriate community but also the more wealthy national families.

Boarding schools overseas

These are very often Christian foundations, multi-national in staff but offering a single nation curriculum (one exception to this being the Kathmandu International Study Centre in Nepal which offers international self-supported study at secondary stage). Some American and Canadian schools also offer the IGCE (International General Certificate of Education), recognising that it provides a broad base for return to US education, and several schools are now offering the French IB (International Baccalaureate).

Boarding schools in home country

These may be secular or religious, and may offer bursaries to families working with charities overseas. They provide continuity with the home system for eventual return.

Home country day school

This involves the student staying with a host family, either friends or relatives, and attending the normal state school at no special cost to the parents.

Home schooling

There are various types of home schooling available and this is a growing market among families from the States. In some cases pressure has been brought upon Europeans to conform to this pattern. It is, however, becoming an increasingly attractive option in Europe, too. The systems include using your own home-produced materials, using a bought curriculum from one of the companies specialising in correspondence courses, which may involve having a tutor back in the home country who assesses the work produced, or corporate home schooling where a group of families get together to home school and share the teaching load between them.

Satellite schooling

This involves having a central point to which all participants relate and refer. Each student is supplied with a computer and work is sent out from the centre of the hub and returned there. The tutor at the hub may go out to visit and monitor the students and groups of students may travel to the hub in order to work together and receive instruction. Various models exist, particularly in Eastern Europe.

Cyber schooling

This is in its infancy but will grow, as has the use of computers in the ordinary classroom learning situation. Students can log on to a program, download their assignment, and email back their work for inspection. Parents can also buy educational packages to take with them and mark themselves, which is really an extension of home schooling.

Advantages and disadvantages

Let's now consider the pros and cons of each method.

National schools

Advantages	Disadvantages
Children stay with their parents	Adjustment to home system
Learn the local language and culture	Take the good and the bad in the host culture
Friends among nationals	Sense of being different from peers
Low cost	Too great identification with local culture/roots
Good standard in many places	Religious/philosophical input
	Quality sometimes is not as good

International schools

Advantages
Living with parents
Western curriculum
Western and national friends
Good adjustment to home culture
Acceptable values (?)
Academically good

Disadvantages
Very expensive
Economic imbalance with peers
Value system (?)
Inappropriate for some non-US
    children

Boarding schools overseas

Advantages
Western curriculum and atmosphere
Good pastoral care
Good adjustment to home culture
Lasting friendships with other TCKs
Relatively near home
Comparatively inexpensive

Disadvantages
Away from parents
Less contact with nationals
Home/parent conflicts
Staffing problems
Sheltered from 'Real Life'

Home boarding schools

Advantages
Compatibility with higher education
Re-entry facilitated
Home curriculum
Contact with other TCKs
Exposure to other activities/
    opportunities

Disadvantages
Extended separation from parents
Cost – fees and travel
Language acquisition unlikely
No friends during vacations overseas
Parents have little control or
    influence

Home schooling

Advantages
Living with parents
More national friends
Knowledge of national culture
Individual or small group instruction
Parental control – input and values
Continuity during home assignments

Disadvantages
Lack of parental skills in teaching
Lack of classroom interaction
Lack of peer/social contact
Problems in evaluating work
Parent-child stress
Time demands on parents
Lack of facilities
Difficulty in transferring later on

Satellite schools

Advantages
Low cost
Continuity with home curriculum
Living with parents
Some interaction with tutor/peers
Supervised and approved curriculum

Disadvantages
Recruitment of personnel
Limited peer contact
Lack of facilities
Limited class interaction

Cyber schools

Advantages
With parents
Flexible study time
Up-to-date material
Low cost
Continuity during home assignments

Disadvantages
Lack of peer/social contact
Limited availability
Lack of practical facilities
Problems in evaluating work
Lack of classroom interaction

Evaluating the methods

The following list of criteria is adapted from a paper given by Alan McIlhenny at a conference on TCKs in 1992 and is reproduced with his permission.

1. Academic credibility – does the system offer an education of comparable standard, covering a comparable range of subjects as is available in the home country? What system is there in place to monitor the academic standards being set? Is there any form of professional educational validation of the material?

2. Cultural dimensions – what allowances does the system make for the student to take advantage of the unique language and cultural environment in which they are placed? What relation do the cultural values of the system have to

Families on the Move

the home as well as the host culture? What is the system of discipline?

3. Spiritual dimension – what is the ethos of the school? Is it one with which you feel comfortable? All systems have a sub-culture, a value system, even if it is not stated. Discover what the ethos is behind the curriculum/system you are considering.

4. Peer interaction – what opportunities are there for your child to interact with his/her peers academically, learning, discussing, competing, experimenting?

5. Social interaction – what opportunities are there for your child to interact socially with his/her peers? Consider sports, arts, clubs and field trips.

6. Parental input – what demands does this system put upon you as parents? If it is over-demanding, parents will end up feeling guilty for not being able to fulfil the demands or for leaving other tasks uncompleted. How much time can you realistically put in? Are there opportunities for you to be involved in class if you want to, e.g. as reading assistants, on parent-teacher bodies etc.? In the case of home schooling, how far can you cope with an intense one-to-one relationship with your child?

7. Professional input – what demands does this system put upon you professionally? Are you professionally competent to deal with those demands? How much will this require of you in training yourself? What other professional input is there? How much homework is required?

8. Meeting re-entry needs – how far does this system fit in with the academic demands of the home country? What degree of continuity is there in the areas of content, order and pace? What is the method of teaching? Is it rote learning? In the area of public examinations, will the qualifications obtainable through this system enable the child to pursue a career in higher education in the home country should he/she desire it?

9. Family togetherness – how far does this system enable you to stay together as a family? If boarding is an option, how many times a year can you afford to bring the child home? Is that sufficient? Is the boarding option in a country other than the home or host country? What will happen during home assignments? Will the child come with you or stay in that third country?

10. Practicalities – how much is this going to cost? Can you afford it? Would you be considering it if you were home with

the same options, living on less money
(or in the case of charity workers,
living on your own funds rather than
the giving of others?). How practical
will it be to continue with this when
you return home, either short- or long-
term?

11. Non-English medium students – does this
system allow you to retain and develop
your mother tongue? Is there allowance
to develop a cultural identity other
than that promulgated by the school?
Can you continue with this system in
some measure during visits home whilst
benefiting from exposure to the home
country's curriculum?

Factors affecting your personal choice

Your child

Each child is different and what is right for one is not
necessarily right for another. At different stages of childhood
development, different strategies may be possible. Some
children have special needs which may dictate the options
open to them. Children who are dyslexic or slow learners
should not be exposed to bilingual education. A very
academically able child needs the right level of challenge and
stimulation in his/her educational environment.

Your own personality

This particularly becomes a factor when considering
home schooling. It is not every parent who can juggle the
roles of parent and teacher satisfactorily – nor can every
child make that distinction. As a teacher, it is important to

retain a degree of objectivity regarding the child you are teaching. If the child in question is your own that can be very hard indeed – particularly if that child has been very difficult and unco-operative in the last twenty-four hours! Home schooling requires definite boundaries both in personal and geographical terms.

I spent some time with Jenny who was preparing to home-school Rebecca because there was no other option. We carefully worked out which would be the school area (not in the child's bedroom), how many hours a day it would take, what curriculum she would use and who would look after the younger child whilst schooling was taking place. On a one-to-one basis, home schooling takes a lot less time than the average school day.

Roots

As with so many of the matters we have considered, the question of where 'home' will eventually be for a child features significantly in the choice of schooling. How far does this option promote your choice of 'home'? Does it leave plenty of options open or does it close the doors on certain courses? Will it facilitate their eventual re-entry or hamper it?

In the case of international schools, parents may well be introducing a third culture into their child's life experience: to what extent will this culture take them over? Can it be counter-balanced by the influence of the home? Does it matter if your children go home with American or British accents which will mark them out from their contemporaries?

The range of options

Depending on your location, the range of options may be large or very limited. Keep an open mind. Past experiences or tales may prejudice us against certain options but it really does help to have no preset ideas so that your evaluation of the options is unbiased.

Lately there has been a swing against the use of boarding schools. But many TCKs I have spoken to have commented warmly on their experiences at boarding school, particularly citing the close friendships they made which endured. One commented: 'I really enjoyed the dorms as I lived with all my friends and did everything with them, making really close friendships.'

They also found the times spent together as a family to be very special, while not denying the pain of separation. One TCK said: 'Separation from my parents at boarding school was obviously the hard bit, but my life was very varied and interesting – overall a positive experience.'

In general, the attitude of the parents was significant in the success of the option. If expressed as a choice rather than an imperative, TCKs felt special and included. Parents often found the separation harder to bear than the children did.

Forward thinking

Look a long way down the line – where is this taking you? The Robertsons were working in North Africa. They decided to put their children in French school all the way. For Jane, this meant going to France for the last four years of study and for Neil going to the capital as a weekly boarder. In addition the family went to France for holidays and only came to the UK to visit relatives for fairly short times. Both children returned to their tertiary education in the UK but they looked French, they dressed French, they spoke English with French overtones.

At the end of their tertiary education both went to live in France and married French partners. The door to the country in which their parents worked was not open to them but in no way did they 'feel' English or wish to settle in England. Their parents are quite comfortable with that decision. But not everyone realises when deciding on total immersion in a culture what the implications are. If you want your children to be able to settle back in your home country, then you need to give them reasonable exposure to it.

Balance of life

Many parents overseas are juggling a number of jobs or roles. There may be the professional role, social demands associated with that role, community involvement, church ministry, care of children under school age (with no local play groups available) housekeeping (which can take a lot longer than expected, even with local help), and the need for personal times of refreshment.

When considering which route to take educationally, the demands that will make on their time and energy need also to be counted. If children are at different schools, on the other side of the city and have to come home at lunch-time, the day is effectively carved out for you. Similarly, those who choose to home school need to take account of the demands and restrictions this puts on their time.

Ethos

This was touched on in 'Evaluating the Methods', but I would like to reinforce it. Parents should investigate the subliminal message the school is sending out and decide whether they are comfortable with that for their child. Even schools which do not claim to be of a particular persuasion do, nevertheless, have an ethos behind their methods of working. If the ethos is in strong contradiction to the ethos of the home, a child will inevitably struggle at being pulled in two directions. It may be that no one school will ever fulfil all our criteria, but the issue should be raised and investigated when making decisions.

Bilingualism

Many TCKs can speak three or four languages without even thinking about it. The problem is that whilst they speak many languages, they can end up being master of none. The advantages of gaining fluency in a second or third language are fairly obvious, but there are other factors to take into consideration.

Most people would agree that to have a conversational ability in the language of the host country is a big advantage when it comes to settling down and feeling part of the community. Language contains many of the nuances of culture, and friendships develop more quickly and more easily where there is a sharing of language. However, it is generally agreed that it takes between one and two years to get a reasonable competence at conversational level.

If the proposed stay is only for a brief spell, parents considering sending their child to a second language school environment need to weigh up the benefits gained from acquiring the second language against the possible traumas the child may experience by being placed in such a different learning environment. Will he/she have time to adapt? What is the age of the child? The younger the child, the easier it is for them to master a new language.

It is important, too, to ascertain the school's and the particular teacher's attitude to having a second language child in the class. David's parents were moving to work in the Netherlands. They were determined to learn the language and settle down there. Both parents booked in for language classes and they decided to send David to Dutch school. They talked the situation through with the staff and both sides were happy. David, aged 5, was the only non-Dutch speaker in his class. The class had two teachers who job-shared. One was prepared to use English with David on

David practised his languages at every opportunity.

Families on the Move

occasions when he didn't understand, the other steadfastly refused to.

One day, David came home in great distress and refused to go to school next day. The whole class had been told to do something and David hadn't understood so hadn't complied with the order. He was then told off for being a naughty boy. As he was generally an obedient child, who liked to do well at school, this hurt. I had Mum on the phone to me. We decided that she needed to go back to the school authorities, particularly the head, who had shown a great deal of sympathy and understanding when they first enrolled, explain the situation and ask if this second teacher could be a little less rigid in her approach. They were not asking for David to get away with anything, just to be given the help and encouragement he needed to do his best. The situation was resolved satisfactorily.

Usually it is not advisable to begin a child in a second language situation after the age of 11 or 12 – back to the dos and don'ts with adolescents. This situation may arise when parents move from one host country to another. In that case, it is best to send the child to a school where the working language is one with which they are familiar, but make arrangements to do conversational classes out of school. You may well find that the school has those classes anyway but by arriving at a later stage the child has missed the elementary stages and needs some private tuition to catch up.

A child who has been educated in a second language environment may give a deceptive appearance of being competent in his/her own mother tongue. But, in fact, although the linguistic fluency is there because it is the language used at home with the parents, the level of literacy may be very much below that expected in the home country. Speaking and writing are two very different matters. One English child who was educated in German said: 'I have always struggled with spelling and grammar due to being confused between two languages.'

When parents are thinking of making the transfer back to the home country for education, whether that be at secondary or tertiary level, they need to ensure that their children have the required level of competence in reading and writing in the mother tongue. For many, this will entail doing some correspondence courses or complementary home schooling prior to return in order to bring the student up to standard.

Sarah was a very bright child who had done well in French school and came back to England to do her GCSEs in one year, having missed the first. She did brilliantly in French but needed some help at the beginning of the course with her essays for the arts subjects – her English just wasn't good enough. Fortunately, the school was able to give her the time and attention she needed. Not all are.

Cultural differences

Some schools overseas require students to repeat a year if they have not spent the previous year in that system. This is a factor to be considered if, say, the family is coming home for a year between assignments. How will that year count on their return if it has been spent in a different system? Schools on the European continent ask students to repeat a year more frequently than they do in England. In Belgium 40% of elementary school-children will repeat a year and 60% of high school students will.

Whatever choice of schooling is made, parents need to recognise that children will need extra support in the initial stages as they are coping with cultural transition in all its manifestations at the same time. It is crucial that the parents' attitude remains positive both to the schooling and to the country. At the risk of repeating myself, the choice needs to be made for each individual child, based on that child's needs.

Susie and her parents had been fortunate enough, or sensible enough, to visit their new country a few months before settling there. They were able to pick out a house and school together. Susie was 10. Within a short time of arriving, Susie showed herself to be very unhappy with her school. She was finding it difficult to make friends and her behaviour in general deteriorated.

She made friends at church with a group of girls who went to the other main international school and pestered her parents to be allowed to change schools. Her parents took notice of her feelings but didn't want to feel they were being pressured or emotionally blackmailed into taking a decision. Together we worked through a list of questions (what other factors were involved, her age, stage of transition, impending birth of new sibling) to discover what lay at the heart of Susie's unhappiness and bad behaviour. When all the possibilities were looked at, they had listened carefully to her complaints and investigated the other school, the decision was made to change schools. There Susie has flourished, her relationship with her parents has been strengthened and the parents feel they have been through a good decision-making process.

Questions

1. What are your priorities for education?
2. What are the options open to you?
3. How far do those options enable you to fulfil the goals you have set?
4. At what stage will your children be when you leave? Do they have any special needs?

5. How long will you spend overseas on this assignment? What are your plans for the time at home between assignments?
6. Where do you foresee your child being able to settle? Does your choice facilitate or place any limitations on that?

 Chapter 7

Living in a Non-Western Culture

Life in Western society is lived at a hectic pace. We are very task-orientated. We are very time-conscious. If we lose our diaries, we lose our life. There is therefore considerable benefit and considerable frustration in moving to a non-Western culture. It can be a very salutary experience for our mental and physical health, providing we also change our mindset from Western to Eastern.

Cultural identification

One of the first questions a family has to ask is, how far is it going to identify with the local culture? The answer to that will depend on a great many things. How long is the proposed length of stay? What is the purpose of the assignment? Does it depend intrinsically on getting to know nationals? How much time is there for language acquisition? How comfortable do they feel with the cultural norms of this society? What, in the long-term, are the implications of immersion in the local culture for the children? Some of these have been discussed in relation to educational considerations but the effect is much wider.

Questions about culture

In order to decide how far one is going to identify with the culture, there are certain questions it is helpful to ask and find the answers to.

1. In this culture, what is the nature of the husband-wife relationship? How much mutual respect is there? What is expected of them?
2. How much freedom does the woman have? What is her acceptable role in society?
3. What is the attitude towards discipline? How are the children taught and disciplined?
4. What part does the father play in the life of a child?
5. How does the family relate to other structures in the society?
6. What are the codes of dress and behaviour that one needs to be aware of and assess the suitability of?

Blending in

Having decided how much of the above is acceptable to them, families then have to work out how they go about changing their lifestyle in order to fit in. A very obvious area is in choice of clothing. In some Islamic societies, for instance, it is very offensive for a woman to wear short skirts, shorts or have bare arms. What is acceptable on the expatriate compound may be an entirely private matter, but to have credibility and status in the local community there is a need to conform to the unwritten code. This will apply to daughters, too, once they reach early adolescence.

If you have daughters, it is well to observe the cultural

norms with regard to their treatment, within reason. In many societies it is not appropriate for adolescent girls to go anywhere unaccompanied. To allow them to do so invites a judgement on their character which is none too favourable. Operating a system of escorting can, however, prove a problem when returning home. Girls may be nervous because they have never been out on their own, but, upon their return, having experienced the freedom of the West, they may find it very irksome to have to be accompanied everywhere.

Food is another area. Is the intention to learn to cook the national way in order to be hospitable to neighbours and the children's school-friends? If so, is the diet acceptable to the family? Do they need to adjust gradually or supplement the diet in order to remain healthy? What about the local water supply? How safe is it?

The ways children find to amuse themselves may well be very different from anything they've had the chance to do before. Parents have to develop a certain insouciance to whatever they may find. Jonathan, aged 11, grew up in Ethiopia and describes his local 'fun' activity:

> In the rainy season we had frog races. We put all the frogs in the centre of a circle and painted their heads to tell which was ours. We waited for one to reach the edge and he was the winner. My little sister squashed one in her tight grip! Once she put my frog in her Postman Pat van.

Ian lived in Liberia. His grandmother probably read the following news with some disquiet: 'We went on a hunt to kill a mongoose that lived under our house. We all made weapons to kill it.'

'In the rainy season we had frog races.'

Language

The issue of language acquisition has already been addressed with respect to making educational choices. However, even if the decision is made not to go for the national school option, there are definite advantages in helping a child to gain a modicum of fluency in a second language.

Here are some TCK comments about the subject:

- 'It allows you to associate with people you wouldn't normally be able to.'
- 'Living in another culture might offer you the chance to learn another language. Indeed, you may have to learn another language, at least a few words, to buy a pizza... or halloumi or pain au chocolat!'
- 'If you know the language you can fit in better.'
- 'I can have more, better friends of people from other countries.'
- 'It gives you skill to learn other languages.'
- 'It will help if I travel.'
- 'It means I can converse more easily, get to know them better on a one-to-one basis as opposed to through an interpreter.'
- 'I strongly recommend that you learn to speak the language of the country you are living in.'
- 'Different languages were easy to pick up' (aged 6).

Notice the frequency of the word 'speak' – it may not be necessary to have the ability to write it.

Total immersion in a new language, however, can cause problems. Hanna was Finnish. She went to English school in the Middle East. Her parents were learning Arabic in order to function in the local community. They had opted for total immersion in the culture. Hanna spoke up one day:

'When am I going to learn enough Finnish to speak to my family back in Finland?'

One family's answer to that dilemma went as follows: 'My parents made sure that we had a specific context for each language. English at home, French at school, German with grandparents and family and Arabic with visitors.'

This complicated situation usually arises when the parents are of different linguistic backgrounds or when the family is working in a team context where the language of communication between team members is neither their own nor that of the host country. Most often it is the non-English speakers who suffer from this scenario.

The pace of life

In most non-Western societies relationships are more important than tasks or time-keeping. If an appointment has been made and someone turns up on the doorstep, one's first duty is to offer hospitality to the guest, even if that means being late for the appointment. There has been much gnashing of teeth on the part of Western executives who have been kept hanging round for an hour or so whilst their contacts fulfilled their social obligations.

There is no point in fighting this – people have to learn to adapt their behaviour accordingly. This means being more flexible in one's schedules and helping children to be so in theirs, and to understand why life does not always run as smoothly as it did at home. There, life revolved around rigid timetables – mealtimes, bedtimes, homework time, and visitors were accommodated around that schedule.

Being on the receiving end of hospitality can be quite a daunting experience as this TCK from Burkina Faso comments:

We spent the night in a compound out in the bush. We arrived in the early evening with the intention of spending the night. Our visit was unexpected and as a result they were not prepared for us. Our dinner therefore was served quite late. We were treated to starters which filled us up and we thought was the whole meal. A couple of hours later, about midnight, they served up a goat which had been killed just for us. We were already full and ready for bed, however, we ate as much as we could. We slept under the stars on straw mats. The night was interrupted twice: once by a goat I found standing over me, and the second time by a herd of cattle which chose to go through the compound in the very early hours.

Just day-to-day living in some societies takes more time. Convenience foods are not available and shopping is done at the local store instead of at an anonymous supermarket. So it is important to greet the shopkeeper, enquire after his family, and he after yours – and so does everyone else in the queue. It can take half the morning to buy the food for supper. Add into that equation the practice of taking a siesta – and it doesn't take long in some places to be convinced of the need to do so – and you have built up a very different lifestyle for you and your family. The next chapter will go on to look at how that will affect your return home.

Attitude to wealth and possessions

Whatever the perception may be of one's station in life when at home, there is no doubt that in many non-Western societies (oil-rich ones excepted) families from Europe will be perceived as wealthy. How can children be helped to handle that and how does the family decide on the lifestyle they think appropriate to the situation? There is a delicate balance between making do with less in order not to offend and maintaining certain standards in order to fit back in when they go home.

One lad remarked:

I was one of only four Westerners in a school of 1,000 boys. Everyone was poor. They called me the 'rich white boy'. I resented that. Didn't everyone know my Dad was a minister? Back home no-one ever called me rich. My parents could never afford to buy all the latest teen fads in brand-name clothes and shoes that created instant status and acceptance at school. Didn't these people understand that?

One day a classmate named Eugene didn't turn up for class. I asked why out loud. Every eye in the class turned to look at me. I was sorry I asked. Later one of my friends explained. Every two weeks Eugene's mother did the wash on Tuesday down at the river. Eugene and his brothers and sisters went bathing while their clothes dried on the rocks. Eugene had only one set of clothes. He was the only one in the family who had shoes, because he went to school.

I went home that day and gazed into my wardrobe filled with clean shirts, jeans, shoes and three full sets of school uniform. I was rich, and I would never again be poor, even if I never owned the perfect psychedelic tie. Slowly I learned to value the person behind the clothes, not the facade, but the real face of the man or woman. Relationships were valued here, not race or rank or remuneration.'

An extreme case? Maybe, but the teenager learned a valuable lesson. A younger child put it like this: 'I learned a lot about poverty because it was all around us. It was not fair for them.'

Possessions can pose a problem too. Traditionally, children are taught at home and at school to share their toys. When someone comes to play, they are expected to play with the other child and give them an equal share in the activity. In some poorer countries, children are not used to having lots of toys around; sticks and stones and perhaps a ball constitute the majority of their playthings. Then a veritable Aladdin's cave turns up when the expatriate family arrives and the child hurls the toys around in delight, having no idea how they are to be properly used.

What strategy is the family going to adopt? Never have any local children around? Allow all the children's treasured possessions to be ruined in the first few weeks? Families find various solutions to this dilemma.

Mary had two small children. She and her husband were determined to be part of the neighbourhood in which they lived. It was a fairly poor one where children were expected to sit around and amuse themselves. They adopted a couple of plans with regard to toys. In the main room was a box of toys which everyone could play with. They were not of any special significance and were, to a degree, expendable. In Lucy's bedroom were her 'special' toys. Friends were invited around to play with them either under supervision or on their own when Mary knew they could be trusted.

She also decided with a friend to run a kind of 'Mums and Toddlers' morning once a week when she invited the ladies around her to come with their children and introduced them to the concept of playing with their children and helping the children to use toys imaginatively. This went down well in the neighbourhood, made for good relationships and protected her children against abuses of their rights.

Security issues

Parents tend to be very security-conscious where their children are concerned nowadays – and rightly so in view of some of the horrific stories that have hit the front pages of the newspapers. Do they anticipate facing the same problems overseas or will things be easier? Or will the problems be different?

This is where there is a need to get the cultural lenses adjusted, to see things from a different perspective but also to be on one's guard against being lulled into a false sense of security often by dint of sheer naiveté.

Touching and being touched

Many non-Western cultures are very tactile – everyone is related in some way, so they all hug each other. Many of us come from a more reserved culture and find that difficult. When is it appropriate for your children to be touched and when is it not?

For white, blond children this can be a source of constant irritation and cause considerable distress. In many communities a child such as that is a rarity, so everyone wants to meet them and touch them. They are perpetually being chucked under the chin, pinched on the cheek and having their hair pulled. This is not done in any unkind way, most of it is quite affectionate. However, for it to happen twenty times a day would be irksome to us as adults, never mind to a 2-year-old who is perhaps strapped into a buggy and has no means of defence! What can parents do to protect their children without causing offence?

At 6 years old, Daniel learned some of the principles of conflict management, not by studying them but by living them. He was attending a local English-speaking school in Batangas and was the only non-Asian in his second year class. One day, when his dad was getting him dressed in his school uniform, he suddenly burst into tears and refused to go to school. It was a shock to Mark because Daniel had always loved school and thrived on learning. Mark made one of those split second decisions parents must make and forced him to go on the school van when it came. He hurt as he heard Daniel's screams as the van headed off. Late in the afternoon I went to his school to talk to his teacher and try to understand what had brought on this outburst.

His teacher said that the other children fought over the privilege of playing with Daniel. They all liked to touch him – his white skin and blond hair were attractive – and they would sometimes pick him up and carry him around like a toy. Daniel was obviously feeling smothered. I also knew from observing that the teachers themselves like to have Daniel to sit on their laps and fussed over him. They gave him great liberty to do as he liked while being strict with the other children.

After asking the teacher to speak to the other children about the problem, I took Daniel for a coke. I asked him specifically how he felt when the other children played with him. He finally opened up and said he didn't like them touching him so much. I told him then that he had to learn to set his own boundaries. He could say to the other children 'Stop touching me so much. I don't like it.' I reminded him that in Canada people didn't tend to touch each other as much as they did in the Philippines. The cultural reality is that he would have to learn to cope with being touched by strangers more than he was used to in Canada. We both learned about the realities of adjusting to a new culture through his experience.

Signs of abuse

I have no intention of setting alarm bells ringing unnecessarily and certainly would not suggest that the incidence or likelihood of abuse is any greater in non-Western cultures than in our own. In Europe we have a sad history recently of cases of child abuse, both physical and sexual, going unheard and undetected for a long time. When overseas, the context in which the abuse occurs may be different and I want to raise the level of parents' awareness so that they can be vigilant.

It is quite common when living in a non-Western culture to have house-helps. A good house-help is a godsend in a labour-intensive environment and often becomes a very good friend of the family. They may in effect become a nanny to the children and hold an important place in their affections. On the whole this is a healthy situation.

However, parents do need to be sure what is happening in the home whilst they are out leaving their children in the care of others. Who visits the house whilst they are out? In cases where children have been abused, it has not usually been the help him- or herself but a relative who comes visiting. In the early days, it is not a bad idea to drop back home unexpectedly when you have left the children with a minder. Also, parents should lay down clear ground rules of what happens during their absence and who may and who may not be allowed in.

It is also sensible to be careful about allowing a child to go and play in someone else's house without accompanying them in the initial stages and making sure of the ground. Really, that applies anywhere. I did hear of one sad story of a child who was sexually abused during a visit to her friend's house. I would not want parents to keep their children in a fortress to which no-one else has entry and from which they have no exit pass. I am merely asking that we are properly vigilant with regard to our children and their safety.

Wherever you are, it is a good idea to familiarise yourselves with the signs a child exhibits when being abused. Children are rarely prepared to come straight out with it verbally. The signals in behaviour come long before that. And they will only speak up if they trust you and feel you will listen to them without being judged. Most charities and organisations have policies regarding child abuse and these include a list of the signs which indicate abuse. Your local school or council may be able to help you with this. There is also a very good Christian organisation called The Churches' Child Protection Advisory Service which has helped both secular and religious organisations in this area and produces excellent guidelines on the subject.

Most parents now teach their children about who may and may not touch them and where they may touch them. If you have not done this before going overseas, or if your child is born overseas, you need just as much to do it there.

Of course, there will probably be the cultural dimension of 'everyone kisses each other on each cheek' (one, two or three times – learn the rule, it depends where you live, even in France!).

Showing affection in public

In the West no-one looks askance at a couple strolling along hand in hand, giving each other the occasional kiss or putting their arms around each other. However, there are parts of the world in which such behaviour is strictly taboo. It may just be frowned upon or there may be a formal reprimand. It is perceived as just another example of decadent Western morals.

The question is, how are you going to respond? Are you going to go ahead and do it anyway and turn your nose up at local culture and customs? Or are you going to conform but maybe find ways around it? What are the acceptable ways of demonstrating affection in this society?

It is possible to walk along together closely without holding hands. To be seen a lot together demonstrates your commitment to each other, particularly in a society where women have an inferior place. For a man to be seen often with his wife demonstrates that he respects her and enjoys having her with him. Within the home, of course, the rules don't apply unless you have visitors. Then you must decide in whose presence it is possible to act naturally without being offensive. Within a short time, most people have developed friendships in which they can be open whilst having acquaintances with whom they have to be more restrained.

In societies such as those described above, it is often taboo for adults to be openly affectionate with children of the opposite sex once they reach puberty. This again calls for sensitive handling. Girls need to know they are loved and appreciated by their fathers, and, whilst such affection can be shown in the privacy of the home, sometimes it's nice for a daughter's friends to see how much she means to her dad and vice-versa. It is a powerful statement, too, if the culture undervalues daughters. Families can get round this by doing more together in public, being seen to be a loving unit. It's not a bad idea either to import the 'group hug' from the States. If everyone is linking hands and hugging together, there's no problem with dad being next to daughter or mother next to son.

Goldfish bowl living

One of the most sought-after prizes at the fair used to be a goldfish in a bowl. Round and round he swam under the eager gaze of his new owner, with nowhere to hide. In many societies, life is lived just like that. It's a far cry from what most Westerners, with their emphasis on privacy and individuality, are used to. There's a saying, 'An Englishman's home is his castle' – I don't know if it has a French or German counterpart but it very accurately describes the British attitude to our homes and families. Once we're inside we pull up the drawbridge and you cross it at your peril. You can come in *if* you have an invitation and prior appointment. Perhaps that's a bit of an exaggeration, but it's not too far from the truth.

In many non-Western societies the cultural norm is to have an open door. People are always dropping in unexpectedly, and because of the culture you are expected to lay aside anything else you're doing in order to make them tea and be generally hospitable. What's more, the questions asked are often intensely personal: 'How much do you earn?' 'Why haven't you any children?' 'Why haven't you *more* children?' Or, in the case of singles, 'Why aren't you married? Didn't your father love you enough to find you a husband? My uncle will help you!'

Moreover, everyone observes you and knows exactly

what you're doing and when, what you've bought and how much you paid for it, who visits you and when, and, if the walls are thin, they know when you have an argument and what gets broken!

Each family has to decide its level of tolerance. A certain amount of adaptation is required if they're not going to fold up completely. If you actually want to get alongside these people and make friends with them, a lot of adaptation will be needed. Because of the need to build a firm foundation for the family, a decision must be made regarding what is priority family time and how it can be preserved. When is the best time of day for it? Is it possible to stay in or do you have to go out? What if you have made a promise to a child and a visitor comes – are you going to break the promise or offend the visitor? Is there any way of compromising? To go on breaking promises to children is to destroy their trust in you. If you go on putting others first, you are lowering the child's sense of worth.

Simon and Helen lived in a villa with walls around it. They had two small children and were the only ex-pats in their area. They decided to turn off the doorbell at a certain time of the day and have family time. It was during midday when a lot of people were eating or sleeping anyway. After a short time, visitors came to realise there was no point in calling at that time because they wouldn't get an answer so they stopped coming. They kept the phone on so that they could be contacted in an emergency.

When it comes to answering the personal questions, it is fairly simple to have the answers worked out in advance. The same old questions will come up time after time in various forms, so a few standard answers will do. Just how much is revealed and how much is withheld has to be a personal decision. Does it matter if they know details of personal finances? If the gulf between what you and they earn is great, it could well sour relations – is it possible to relate it in terms of what it is used for? For example, 'I earn enough to rent this house, send my children to school, feed the family and go home to visit my parents once a year.'

Family is very important in such societies, so spending money to see them or bring them out to see you will meet with general approval. Talking of family size may well help them to think about the same issues for themselves, particularly in a society where having children, especially sons, is seen as a sign of virility. The women are often keener on family planning than the men, so a little support doesn't go amiss!

Once parents have worked out their own answers, they can start helping the children work out how they're going to respond to similar questions and how much it will be prudent for them to divulge. Children are usually more open and honest about their dealings (and yours, if you've ever read their school diary!) so they generally won't have such a problem. It may be more of a problem in teaching them what not to say, especially if the situation is in any way security-sensitive.

Avoiding health risks

Assuming that all the requisite injections to prevent disease have been given, what else can be done to minimise further risk?

Few people realise that there can be as much danger to their health from accidents as from illness. Driving in certain countries can be a hazardous activity:

I was travelling with my mother and two sisters in a taxi that had definitely seen better days. The usual conversation started between my mother and the elderly Sikh who was driving us. 'These are your daughters?' 'Yes.' 'And have you any sons?' 'No.' 'No sons! I will pray to God for you to have sons!' At which point he took both hands off the steering wheel and clasped them as if to pray. The only snag was that we were just coming on to a roundabout!!

It is vital that parents always wear their seat belts and insist that their children do so no matter whose car they may be travelling in. In many cultures seat belts either do not exist or are totally ignored. If the car you purchase doesn't have them, do your utmost to get them fitted.

If you are a passenger, make sure your driver is not under the influence of alcohol or any other substance. Learn a few pithy, humorous phrases to use when your taxi or rickshaw driver is driving too fast or with no regard to safety – you may divert him from his chosen course of action.

Avoid driving at night on unknown and dangerous or unmade roads. Make sure you are not suffering from tiredness. Watch how you walk as a pedestrian and take care to teach your child good road safety procedures, especially in a country where no-one pays much attention to the rules of the road!

Avoid swimming accidents by teaching your children not to run along slippery edges, not to swim out of their depth and not to swim in local waters. In general the sea is OK but local rivers, lakes and swamps may prove breeding grounds for Bilharzia.

Malaria is still a big risk and in many areas is resistant to Chloroquine. In areas where it is a risk families should be vigilant in their use of mosquito nets, make sure they are regularly treated with repellent, use insect repellents and cover up in the evening and persist with anti-malarial tablets, even if you have friends who scorn the idea.

Wherever they are, children run the sorts of risks which prematurely age their parents. Alison grew up in Ethiopia:

We lived on a large compound with several other families. One day our 7-year-old neighbour came running to my mum

'Learn a few pithy, humorous phrases to use when your taxi is driving too fast.'

because Zachary (18 months) was right at the top of a tree, having climbed up a ladder left there. I was scared. My mum had to climb up and get him down.

Western teenage norms

This subject will be covered more fully in the next chapter on re-entry. However, I would like to mention at this point that the sexual norms may be very different in the country where the TCK is growing up from those back in the home country. What are the moral norms where he/she is living? A boy may have very little contact with girls once in adolescence if he attends national school. If he is deep into the interior of the country he may not be fazed by bare-breasted women. If a child is at boarding school, he or she may be under very strict supervision and in a protected environment.

Before going home, parents need to analyse the differences between life as the child has known it and life as they will meet it on return.

Discipline

How we discipline our children is frequently a source of conflict, between husband and wife, between neighbours, between friends and colleagues, and, once you get overseas, between cultures. In the sort of society where sons are important it is quite common for young boys to go totally undisciplined. They are the apple of their mother's eye and can do nothing wrong. Having a son has brought her prestige and value in the sight of her husband and neighbours. This is true not just of poor families but throughout the strata of a society with such values, so it will be true of the wealthy as well.

The tension comes when either you are visiting their house or they are visiting yours. Where do you draw the line? Do you have house rules that apply to anyone who visits? Can you sensitively lay them down on the first visit so that there is no confusion but equally in such a way that you do not cause offence?

Parents may well find, however, that the greatest tension comes not with national families but with the families with whom they are working or in community. This is particularly so in a team-work situation. We tend to be very critical of how others bring up their children. There is often a noted divide between North American and European. In such a situation, you need to work through these areas carefully, without making judgements and with a fair degree of tolerance.

It is also vital to have some clues to the sexual norms of the society in which you are living and be able to match them up against your own. I heard a story of a child attending an international school who came home one day to tell his parents that a teacher had been touching his private parts. His parents, in great distress, went to the school to find out what was happening. On closer investigation they discovered that it was the cultural norm in that country to discipline small boys by touching their private parts – the teacher couldn't see that she had done anything wrong, she certainly had no intention of abusing or harming the boy. A process of education went on and eventually the teacher was restored to her position. Who in the school hadn't done their cultural homework?

If parents want to maximise for both themselves and their children the benefits of living overseas, then they need to make changes to their lifestyle and thinking. They need to suspend judgement on what is good and what is bad, culturally speaking. The West has a lot to learn from the East in the matters of personal relationships, valuing people more than things, appreciating the elderly and the continuing contribution they have to make and living life at a more measured pace that doesn't burn us out. If people can make those changes, change the cultural lens through which they view the world whilst not suspending their critical faculties, the whole experience will be one that enriches and strengthens both them and their children.

Questions

1. How can you give your children adequate attention when you are constantly overlooked or have constant visitors in a culture where visitors always have priority?
2. Where can you find mentors for yourself and your children who will help you through the cultural maze? What will you ask them?
3. How can parents train their children without causing serious misunderstanding in a culture where the training of young children is not thought necessary?
4. How do you help a child cope with/react to the situation of being constantly touched and fussed because he is white?
5. In a culture where it is taboo to show affection in public, how can a family build a sense of love and affection?
6. In a people-intensive culture people make many shallow relationships but few deep ones. Deep relationships may be viewed with suspicion or embarrassment. How can a Western family cope with this?

▶ Chapter 8

Re-Entry

When I found out we were leaving India, I was excited at the thought of all the new people, good food and rock music I would encounter! I was a little sorry to say goodbye to my friends, but I had absolutely no concept of what I would go through once I returned home.

After the first day or two, I felt a sudden sense of loss. I simply had no one to talk to and everything was strange and alien. All I did was cry, listen to music and write hundreds of unposted letters.

Slowly and painfully I have made friends and become less culturally ignorant. But especially in the first months, I felt as if everyone I knew had died. I cried constantly over photos and letters and became extremely sick of meeting new people.

Kate, a TCK who grew up in India

From feelings like that it is a very small slide to serious depression unless someone is on hand to listen and pick up the pieces. In the past, preparation was given to families going overseas for the first time, but re-entry was seen as a non-event. After all, the family was coming home. What organisations failed to realise was that for most TCKs the opposite was true – they were not coming home, they were leaving home.

Peter described it like this: 'I felt culture shock on

return to a strange place called home. People assume that somewhere overseas is an alien place, but home is often the strangest.'

Here's another comment: 'The country where I am living now is, after all, not home, even though it is my passport country. I long to continue travelling.'

Even parents are not returning to the familiar – places have changed and so have people; the town centre is gone, all the shopping is out of town, the houses have been pulled down and the school has shut; the hospital where you gave birth to your child has closed down. For children who have grown up overseas, there is nothing they can expect to be familiar, they have no memories associated with the place. All their memories, signposts, places of residence, study, and entertainment are elsewhere.

Culture shock has been described as primarily an emotional reaction that follows from not being about to understand, control and predict another's behaviour. One TCK comments: 'I didn't know my parents' language well enough to relate ideas or beliefs.' Even if you do know the language, you may not be sufficiently au fait with the culture to pick up the unspoken signals being sent to you.

We have already remarked on the stress associated with transition, and that is intensified in re-entry by the loss of all that is significant in a person's life – there are no recognisable landmarks. Just as on a road journey you look for familiar sights to know you are on the right road, so we all, consciously or subconsciously, rely on daily routines, encounters, and places to give us a frame of reference for our lives, a sense of meaning. Without them we are plunged into chaos and confusion.

Chaos and confusion quickly move into anger and depression, anxiety about whether we will be able to cope, wondering if we will ever manage to fit in. Listen to this comment:

I was only about 9 when we went back for good but I had very strong feelings about leaving friends and the country I'd come to see as my home. It took quite a while to adjust to such a different atmosphere and to stop feeling homesick. I think adults just need to be aware that children have the same capacity for emotion.

Similarly, this:

I wondered why did we have to go to England because I didn't feel I knew anybody there and my friends were in Ethiopia. I was devastated – sad, lonely, angry at God for not giving us a work permit to stay. I was deeply upset and cried quite a lot.

There are various factors that will affect how a child responds to the experience of re-entry. For the purposes of this chapter, re-entry refers to a return to the home country for the foreseeable future. For the majority of TCKs this happens at or near the stage of tertiary education, by which time they are able to process a lot of what is happening to them if they are given help and a good debriefing. We will consider ways of doing that later and of helping younger children to cope with the stress of saying goodbye.

Factors affecting re-entry

Age

When looking at the Transition Experience it was noted that there are certain times in a child's life when moving is to be avoided if at all possible. What age will your child be when you move? Where is that in the life cycle of a child, what stage of development is it? Is the child old enough to understand what is happening? How have you tried to convey what this move means? With older children, how much have they been involved in the decision-making process?

Individual personality

As so often, each child is a unique individual in his or her own right, with his or her own background and experiences. How would you describe your child in personality terms? How deep are the relationships he/she has formed? Is he/she the sort of person who makes friends easily? Is he/she at heart a pessimist or an optimist – is their glass always half-full or half-empty? How much does he/she talk about how they're feeling?

Julia commented: 'No-one understands if I try to tell them what it's like, so I don't bother.'

Previous experience of moving

What a child has learned from its previous experiences very much colours its attitude to this move. Think back. What did your child feel about the last move – was it a good or bad experience? How many times have you moved in this child's lifetime? What was the total experience of the multiple moves?

Reasons for leaving

Why is this move necessary at this time? The philosopher Friedrich Nietzsche said, 'I can stand any "how" if I have a "why".' If someone in the family is ill, then that's understandable. If a point is reached in education when there really is no alternative but to return home, that is also comprehensible. However, sometimes parents take children home in preparation for re-entry at tertiary level but it means they have to miss out on the last year at school, which is often a high point in a child's school career and one they have looked forward to for years.

One family said that their agency had told them that the local education system was not valid in the UK so they would have either to return at secondary school level or send their children to British boarding schools. They came back. In fact, that information was quite erroneous – I knew of a girl, educated in that system, who had obtained a place at Cambridge University to study for her degree.

Disappointment, frustration and misunderstanding on this point can be avoided if parents talk the plan through with the child concerned well before it is put into operation. With the best possible intentions they may be doing some things that the child will resent for a long time to come and blame them for because they were not privy to the reasoning behind the decision.

In the case of crisis evacuation, no-one has any say in the matter and though the reason may be apparent, there is no way of preparing the child for re-entry or handling the accompanying stress. There is no way to plan the timing, the means of going or the ultimate destination. Most organisations with workers overseas do have good crisis contingency plans so that there is a recognised course of action to follow should such an eventuality occur.

Ian, who spent four years in Liberia and four years in Ethiopia, says: 'It was very hard for me to adjust to the English system at school. I got teased a lot for having an American accent and called names like "refugee" because I had been evacuated. I wanted to go back home.'

Cultural perceptions

This goes back to the question of roots. We know that a TCK doesn't feel he/she belongs anywhere but we have also discussed the need to give them some sense of cultural identity to make it possible for them to settle somewhere, given that rarely is it possible for a TCK to settle in the country where their parents have been working.

Philip says: 'The only thing I really feel I missed out on was "belonging somewhere" – when I came back I felt a bit rootless and I envied other British kids who were *from* somewhere.'

Anne remarks: 'I found it hard being out of touch with "home"; I never really knew all that much about where I was supposed to be from.'

Daniel comments: 'I totally missed out on the English "culture-thing" and was utterly devastated when I arrived in England at 11. However, I recovered *after 2 years*, and school was a blast.'

In the case of cross-cultural marriages particularly, this may remain an unresolved issue. To discuss the pros and cons of one culture against another and to decide that one rather than the other will be the principal home, thus cutting off contact in large measure with the other country, the family left behind there, the customs and things special to you in it, is a painful process and many couples avoid it for too long for that precise reason.

Their uncertainty is then passed on to the child who may not know until the last minute, or last twelve months, where he or she will eventually end up. At that stage it is too late to build into the life experience the bridges spoken about in chapter five.

Attitude of parents

Children are quick to pick up the vibes of how parents feel about any situation or prospective move. It is both the attitude to leaving and the attitude to the new environment which will affect the children. Is there a sense of relief in this situation? Are there tensions and stresses they will be glad to leave behind?

Is it a decision you deeply regret and is sadness the overwhelming emotion you feel now? What about the situation into which you are entering, how do you feel about that? Are you going grudgingly? Is there anxiety and uncertainty about what the future holds? Parents who display a degree of confidence in change, encourage their children to feel confident too.

Julia (aged 21) comments: 'My parents are both very practical and realistic, which has helped with the different adjustments. The children, at least in my experience, usually adapt very fast, but it's the parents who hold them back.'

Economic diversity

For some children, returning home means returning to a land of wealth, a place where materialism reigns supreme, where the shops are full of goods undreamt of in their host country. There is a bewildering array of choice all around them. One TCK spoke of having a great time in the 'rich West'. Suddenly from being the wealthy foreigner, they are conscious of being the pauper in this society. Their clothes are not up to date with the latest designer labels and what they could have bought for a few pence now costs a few pounds, dollars or euros.

Conversely, some children have grown up overseas in a very affluent environment. One family I knew were overseas because the father was church minister to an oil company. The perks of the job included a house with a swimming pool, a car and chauffeur and a maid and a house boy. Returning to a similar job in England meant considerable downsizing.

Sometimes the sizes of salaries overseas, the low taxes, the low cost of daily living expenses has meant that there is a lot of spare cash to spend on yourselves and your children. It has been nothing to own a boat, have membership of a club, riding lessons, and the prospect of eating out regularly. According to which end of the scale you find yourselves, the response from your children will be very different.

Educational context

At what point in a child's schooling do you decide it is time to make a move, assuming that the decision is up to you? This question is more complicated than it sounds. Most people would say it is when there is a natural break in their schooling, the move from junior to secondary school, before or after public examinations. The problem is that most families have more than one child. Whose interests do you put first? If you move when it is right for the eldest child, perhaps just after public exams, you may be moving a younger child in the middle of a course of study. This is where it is important to know your child and who can best cope with the upheaval if it cannot be at a time that is ideal for all.

Debrief

It is essential that the whole family on return to the home country has the opportunity for a proper debrief. This gives all members an opportunity to express and acknowledge their feelings, to process the loss and deal with the grief. They need the presence and help of people who understand the issues relating to cultural transition and, in the case of TCKs, of the Third Culture Kid experience. Above all, there is a need for people who will listen, not advise, cajole, or downplay what they are feeling.

The diagram of the bridge is one way of creatively exploring the various emotions and responses that TCKs have when facing re-entry, both before, during and immediately after. It seeks to creatively allow them to express the feelings they have and to stimulate ways of handling those feelings.

The bridge diagram

Some years ago Simon and Garfunkel had a hit record with a song entitled 'Bridge Over Troubled Water', and when introducing this diagram to a group of TCKs I would play this record. The words used evoke many of the feelings TCKs experience on their return – 'when you're weary, feeling

THE BRIDGE

Alien
Disorientated
Unknown
Sorrow
Foreign
Strange
Rejection

Appropriate skills

People to listen

Watching and listening

Anticipation

Grieving

Realistic expectations

Forward planning

Good closures

Extended family
Mentors
Local support

Uncertainty
Anxiety
Doubt
Depression
Insecurity
Loss
Fear
Vulnerable
Powerless

Parents
Friends
School
Local community

Known
Security
Contented
Happy
Safe
Familiar
Accepted
Comfortable
Nervous

small…when times get rough and friends just can't be found…when darkness comes and pain is all around'. I would then ask them how many of those sentiments they can identify with and encourage them to elaborate. We would then work our way through the bridge diagram. This is put up on a flip chart for a brainstorming exercise and each individual would have his/her own copy to work on in private first.

Initially the stones of the bridge, the supporting pillars and the waters are blank. Onto the ground of the host country can be written the words expressing how the TCK feels before leaving; these will be words like 'secure', 'safe', 'known', 'comfortable'. On the opposite side are words describing how they feel about the new environment; these will be words like 'unknown', 'alien', 'rejected', 'disoriented'. Across the waters can be written the feelings they experience when in transition; these will be words like 'uncertainty', 'fear', 'anticipation', 'excitement', 'resentment', 'depression'.

There is then the opportunity to fill in the blocks of the bridge, identifying measures or steps that enable someone to make a safe crossing over the troubled waters. The supporting pillars can be filled in, naming the people and networks which give, and will give, foundations for survival. After filling in the stones, the following questions might prompt a creative way to think further through the process:

- How wide is the bridge? How far does it reach?
- Does it feel like a tightrope?
- Is it swaying, like a suspension bridge?
- Who will be there on the other side?
- Whom have you left behind?
- If you lose your balance, are there any rescue boats?
- What can you take with you?
- Climbing up the bridge – how much of the other side can you see?

- What sort of signposts are there to see where it's leading?
- Is anyone else going with you?
- What are the main supports at each end of the bridge?

Summary

At the time of re-entry there is a sense of loss in all spheres of life – physical, emotional, material and spiritual. This sense of loss often leads to an inability to function in normal everyday life. The TCK's comments quoted at the beginning of the chapter are not untypical.

A 22-year-old says:

> I found it hard as I was totally different from other kids; I looked, dressed, spoke and thought different. I tried to fit in and make friends, though my friendships weren't that deep. In general I have a real problem with commitment as I am always prepared to move on to another place.

Small problems assume enormous importance. Decision-making becomes impossible. The TCK may be uncertain of what to do and not know who to turn to ask. The usual supports have been pulled from under his feet. This is of course exaggerated when the TCK is sent home for further education either unaccompanied by a parent or only accompanied for a short time and no parent-substitute is in place.

Eva spells this out: 'When I returned I had an unrealistic fear of my classmates – that I would be bullied at school, that people swore all the time and were particularly nasty! This, I think, came from the books I read!'

It is an immensely tiring time. Coping with this transition takes a lot of effort and involves a lot of stress. Just living from day to day is stressful, especially if adequate preparations have not been made. The TCK may never have been truly independent before. All children have a degree of insecurity when they first leave home, but for most of them the safety net of the parental home is only a phone call and a matter of miles away. For some TCKs it is on the other side of the world!

Re-entry is often accompanied by a strong sense of alienation and isolation. The returning TCK looks as though he ought to fit but doesn't feel as though he fits. He looks like everyone else, so everyone assumes he knows the ropes whereas in fact he feels like a foreigner. The TCK then feels increasingly isolated by his situation; he finds it difficult to be part of his peer group, his sense of values is very different and his history is too. He may actually reject his new culture, comparing it unfavourably to the one he has left, and if he is vocal with his disapproval he will soon end up alienating his mono-cultural peers who have never known anything different.

Elaine, who spent 18 years overseas, describes her experience at university:

> I got on OK with people my own age at university but found it difficult to develop any depth of relationship as I felt they couldn't really understand me. A university friend whom I met some years later commented that they had all liked me but didn't understand me!

Because the TCK belongs everywhere and nowhere, this stage is marked by feelings of confusion with regards to his sense of identity, his value system, and the expectations of himself and of others. Who is the TCK expected to be – by his peers, his parents, his tutors? Who does he feel himself to be? Who does he want to be? Where are his role models? How should he judge this society, its behaviour, its patterns, its people? What is to be his yardstick?

The frustration involved in coping with the process can result in anger, resentment and anxiety. The TCK may feel betrayed by those he loves for putting him in this situation. Anger can come because he feels he has no control of the situation and there is no way he can see to gain control – it is spiralling away from him.

Anxiety comes from the uncertainty. What if he doesn't make it in the first year, what if he never fits in? Where can he go to next? Who can possibly understand what it is like for him?

Without the right strategies in place, the TCK may become incapable of functioning at the level of 'normal', routine life. This is a worst case scenario, but to some degree it is one which all TCKs face. So what strategies can be put in place to make this a more conducive experience?

Preparation

Eliminate unnecessary stress

Get as many practical things into place as early as possible before departure. For TCKs coming home to college this means finding out the courses open to them, the entry requirements, the financial implications, the application forms and the dates by which applications have to be submitted. Local consulates and embassies overseas should be able to help with providing that information.

If the children will be of school-age, parents need to know how long before coming home they need to be enrolled in the local school. Also, is there a choice of schools? Which would suit them best?

It is important as a prior step to find out what career choices the TCK has in mind. Career opportunities and courses may exist of which he knows nothing. Does the school he attends overseas have a careers advisor? If so, is that advisor familiar with the requirements of the home country? If there is no-one in that capacity, who can help them? Is there an opportunity to get career aptitude tests from the home country to complete whilst overseas, send home and obtain results?

Where will you be based on your return? How temporary will that be? What is the prospect of finding somewhere permanent within a reasonably short space of time? What sort of accommodation is available at the place of study you have chosen? How much does it cost?

Teach appropriate skills

This can be anything from table manners for a 7-year-old to opening a bank account for an 18-year-old. Your child may always have eaten with his fingers and run around with no shoes on. Grandma may find this highly undesirable, so it is as well to teach the child how to hold a knife and fork, how to lay a table, what to expect as sauces or accompaniments to meals, or anything else you anticipate him encountering with which he is unfamiliar.

Children who have been to boarding school may have no idea how to wash a shirt, cook a meal, clean a room or find their way from A to B. A few basic lessons in household management will go down a treat with their new flatmates.

It may never before have been possible for a TCK to have a credit card, a switch card or a cheque book. How much experience have they had of budgeting, balancing an account, paying for phone calls, paying to go out socially? In other words, the whole area of financial management. They need to know the implications of running up large credit card bills and the effects of the mounting interest.

Most young people in the home country will have had the opportunity of holding down Saturday jobs or holiday jobs as a means of earning some extra cash. The TCK may have had no experience in this area and no idea of how to

Learning appropriate table manners.

go about getting temporary employment to help see him through his college course.

TCKs may need help in mastering study skills. For instance, how to manage their time, if it has always been managed for them at boarding school; how to use a library, if your local school had limited facilities; how to use a computer, though most families now have access to one personally even if the school does not possess any.

Find mentors in the peer group

You think it's just another move and you'll be the new one and therefore it's OK to be ignorant, but to the kids in Canada, I was coming home and therefore I should know! They really thought I was stupid. Get to know the in-jargon from someone.

At first, until you adapt, you may get called a NERD.

When I first got back I found it fairly difficult to make friends. A lot of people called me French, which I didn't enjoy.

I definitely lacked any sense of fashion when I returned. And since being in England, I am always stuck when the conversation turns round to what kids' programmes people used to watch, or certain music bands I was unaware of since I was in Pakistan at the time.

TCKs need mentors of their own age group who will be the culture-brokers into the new society. They want to know about the climate and the clothing; the sports and current events; the pop music and the latest 'in' words and expressions. Don't wait till they get home to find these things out. Make contact with someone well before you leave who will write (or, more likely, email) to answer those questions and send some magazines or appropriate articles.

When they get home, they'll need someone who will

take them around and introduce them to society, someone who will let them just watch and listen in. Someone to take them to the Quasar place, the disco, bowling alley or multiplex cinema. It helps to know the score on who pays for things, when you're expected to treat someone, how much to spend on a birthday present, how much an evening out can cost.

Decision-making

Before coming home, help your TCK to think through how he makes decisions. Ask these sorts of questions:

- What are your long-term goals?
- What are the options open to you?
- What is important to you?
- What will it cost?
- What are the consequences of this decision?
- What degree of commitment does this take on your part?
- How do you rate your choice?

For TCKs who often see marriage and commitment as a cure for homesickness, the ability to think through the implications of decision-making and to take responsibility for those decisions is vital.

Handling crises

Make sure your TCK knows where he can go to for help when in a crisis situation. This can range from serious situations like rape, robbery, lost documents, feelings of suicide to practical things like where to spend the holidays if mum and dad are overseas and you can't afford to get there, getting low grades and feeling discouraged, running out of money or being ill. TCKs should be warned against the danger of cults. When they feel isolated they are very vulnerable to the sense of community which these cults offer. They should be warned against anything which seeks to isolate them further from their community and their family.

Make good closures

When we looked at the transition experience, we looked at the importance of saying goodbye properly – here is where it comes into its own. As Dave Pollock says, 'Without a meaningful goodbye and effective closure there cannot be a creative hello and a new beginning.'

It is important to take the time to do the round of goodbyes, particularly with a child who may never have the opportunity to return, for whatever reason. Many TCKs decide to take time out after a college course to revisit all the places that were precious to them during their growing up years. They feel there is a sense of completeness in being able to say goodbye again once they have made the adjustment back into a home culture. It helps make a connection between the past and the present.

This observation is fairly typical: 'I would certainly like to go back to Ghana or at least Africa at some point – even just a few months spent with an overseas development programme.'

A TCK I know, who had grown up in Zambia, returned to South Africa after her college course because she needed to 'get Africa out of her system'. Three years on she is still living and working there!

Practical ideas for re-entry

Creative listening

Most TCKs find it hard to talk about what they are feeling. The subject is too painful, the emotion too strong and the grief too new. There is a need to find creative ways of listening, through craft work, collages and cartoons;

through drama and role-play; through the writing of stories, poems and letters; through other forms of artwork.

Small children may be helped with the use of puppets because in telling a story through a puppet they can supply the words for the way the puppet is feeling about what is happening to him. This way they both express and transfer their emotions. There is an excellent book entitled *Harry and Stanley say Goodbye* by Jill Dyer about a family of teddy bears and their experience of moving. It's an excellent one to read through with small children and to help them to talk.

Keeping a diary is a good way of expressing feelings in private. But a personal log book or diary should be just that – personal. TCKs need to know that their privacy is respected and that no-one else will take the liberty of reading their private writings. Even if correspondence with friends lapses, an imaginary correspondence can continue in the diary.

Keeping in contact

TCKs used to keep the postal service in business – now they just tie up the internet connection! They don't usually have to be told to get the addresses of all their contacts but a gentle nudge wouldn't go amiss. It's good to encourage them to write cards or send messages to those who have been significant in their lives before they leave, and again when they have returned home.

Be prepared for some large travel bills. Since TCKs have friends all over the world and enjoy keeping up with each other, they are keen to attend weddings, birthdays, christenings and any other occasion that's a good excuse for getting together.

Photos

By the time he returns, the TCK may well have a suitcase bulging full of photograph albums. If this is to be the last move, make sure there are plenty of shots of all the people and places that are important in his life. Arrange to have some blown up and framed to hang on the wall of his bedroom or college study.

When you have returned, make sure he sends back photos of his new situation to the people he has left behind. As with the bridges that were built when first going overseas, it is important to preserve a sense of continuity upon return, not to burn the bridges behind you.

Debrief

If possible, either privately or through the organisation, arrange a proper debriefing session. Work through the bridge model with someone who understands. Try to educate the people you are returning to, your family, organisation, friends, church, about what is happening. People can be very insensitive and think it's just great for you that you've come home, and aren't you lucky?

In reality, parents and children are going through a bereavement and need the time to grieve. Leadership roles are often thrust upon people making a return when what they need is time and space apart to reflect. TCKs, too, need the opportunity to reflect on what has happened. They may not find ready listeners amongst their peers so the parents may need to seek out people who can come alongside them and listen.

The most appropriate analogy today for re-entry is that of the spacecraft. Will it burn up or splash-down? The space authority does everything in its power to ensure it makes a safe splash-down. The timing of the re-entry and the trajectory to make sure it hits at the right point are all carefully calculated. Everything is on standby to receive the returning astronauts. There's a parachute to make sure the landing isn't too bumpy. No-one expects the ride to be comfortable but the discomfort is minimised and all is ready in the recovery suite to ease the astronauts back into normal gravity.

The comparison to the TCK making re-entry doesn't need labouring. Parents and receivers need to do their utmost to set up the ideal scenario and guide the returning TCK to a safe splash-down – they deserve it!

Questions

1. What are the three things you will miss most when you return 'home'? What are the three things you most fear facing?
2. What arrangements have you made to say goodbye? Who do you need to say goodbye to?
3. What arrangements have you made to keep in contact? How can you store your memories?
4. How much do you know about the country to which you are returning? Can you name the prime minister, top team, pop group? Where can you find such information?
5. What do you currently do for recreation? What does your peer group back 'home' do to relax? How will you fit in?
6. Are there any practical skills you need to acquire before/when you return? Who can help you? Who will you trust with your confidences?

▶ Chapter 9

Overseas on Vocation

F or many families, going overseas is a matter of taking up a foreign posting or agreeing to undertake an overseas assignment. Some may be forced to look elsewhere for a job after being made redundant in their home country or there may just be better opportunities to use their skills overseas. If you are in that category, then this chapter may not be relevant to you, and I trust you've found the rest of the book helpful.

The majority of my past experience, however, has been with families who fall into the category of those going overseas because of a sense of call, of Christian vocation. For them, the actual job is subservient to the ministry to which they feel called. If you fall into that category, then read on – there's more to come. I have said very little about the spiritual dimension so far, beyond encouraging you to check the second culture and the ethos of the school curriculum against your own beliefs and values.

The spiritual dimension will affect how you view your assignment, how you perceive your role and how your children perceive your work. They are part of a much bigger package. Within this experience they can not only mature physically and emotionally and derive all the other benefits of being a TCK, they can also grow spiritually as they experience God's care and provision.

But there are challenges, too. One comes if children ever think that they have been sacrificed to the needs of the ministry, that they take second place in the family's thinking. For that reason, my first challenge to you is to consider the Family *in* Ministry, not the Family *or* Ministry.

In the past, Christians have left all and gone overseas in response to a call, and not allowed anything or anybody to interfere with that call. There were many TCKs who felt themselves to be 'victims'. Decisions had been taken over their heads, they were given short notice of changes to be made and were encouraged to maintain a stiff upper lip and not show their emotions – the work of the Kingdom was more important than they were.

The corollary to this is that if the experience doesn't work out for them and they feel angry, resentful and aggrieved, there is only one person whom they can blame for it – God. He issues the call, he guided parents into the course of action (or so they've been told) and he is the sovereign. This is not the best way of fulfilling Psalm 78:4: 'We will tell the next generation the praiseworthy deeds of the Lord, his power and the wonders he has done.'

When God calls someone to serve him overseas, his call is to the whole family. If they are childless at the time, or single, he has in mind, too, the potential family they may have. Having children does not surprise him! Ephesians 3:15 talks about the 'Father in heaven from whom every family in heaven and on earth receives its name'. In the Bible, 'name' means character; the character of family is in the nature of God, so it should develop according to his character, that is, loving, giving, caring.

The matter of call is extremely important when the going gets tough. At the stage of selection I have noticed an increase in couples where the wife says, 'My husband is called and I'm going because I'm called to be his wife.' Unless both partners are committed to the calling, it will become a source of friction within the marriage. Whenever hardship arises, the wife can say 'I wouldn't be here if it weren't for you.' A wife can become introverted, tuned in only to life as it affects her and have no contact with her husband's ministry. In cultures where hospitality features large in ministry, this is a real drawback.

Children, too, need to perceive the worth of their parents' work. Decisions taken with regard to ministry and assignments affect them deeply. If parents spend a lot of time criticising co-workers, nationals or the sending agency, then children are entitled to ask the question 'Why bother? What am I doing here?'

Family in ministry means getting the balance right, learning when to say 'no', prioritising family time. Many of those who go overseas with a call are driven people; they have goals to aim at and are task-orientated. There's a lot riding on their ministry and most are dependent on the gifts of fellow-Christians at home to keep them overseas. There is, then, a sense of obligation, of stewardship.

One TCK writes:

Surprisingly enough, it was during the MK (Missionary Kid) stage that I resented my parents for taking us away from all the creature comforts and civilisation, and their not having enough time for us. I blamed it on their calling and really avoided Christianity until the Diplomat stage. At this stage I was old enough to create a life of my own and their job did not affect it. I could choose Christianity, whereas before I had no choice, and so I did.

Family in ministry means taking into account the needs of the whole family when making decisions. It means involving young children, up to the age of ten, in the planning process, and over the age of 10, in the decision-making process itself. There are things you can do with small children that are inappropriate with teenagers. There are times when a family needs to say 'no' to an assignment, however strong the pressure from the sending agency may be. Similarly, at the selection stage, it is sometimes good care to refuse a family because of the brokenness that could result.

Prioritising family time means being available to watch your child in a soccer match or the school play. It means making the time to write or phone regularly if they're away in boarding school. One boarding school head said, 'One of my major tasks is to convince parents that admissions papers are not the same as adoption papers.' A couple I know who run a hostel for TCKs say that they have had to write to parents and ask them to contact their children as nothing has been heard from them for weeks.

Making commitments to be part of their lives helps children to know that they are valued. It is not enough to say 'I love you,' they have to see that love in action. Children also perceive that they are valued when they are included in decision-making and planning. Knowing that there are educational options for them is another factor. It is important that children never feel that the door is closed on them, that they have no choice. One TCK who had been through boarding school told me: 'I could stand it because I knew that if ever I needed to, my parents would come and pick me up as soon as I phoned.'

Another said: 'My parents told me I could choose to go to boarding school, and I felt privileged to be able to do so.'

Both had very positive views on the boarding school experience.

Coping with stress

As has been said, a certain amount of stress is inevitable in growing up. The important thing is to separate the normal childhood stresses from the cultural ones. Overlying that, too, can be the stress of not being willing to upset one's parents' ministry in any way by complaining of how it affects you. Some TCKs who were abused at a Christian boarding school kept quiet for many years because their abuser told them that they couldn't tell anyone or their parents would have to leave the mission field. Obviously, we should nurture the sort of relationship with our children where they feel free to tell us anything without fearing we will be shocked or outraged. They need to be able to share their pain as well as their pleasure with parents.

A certain amount of stress and pressure is healthy and helps us to grow. We are in danger in the West of being overprotective of our children. Children are becoming fatter and at greater risk of being unfit because they are no longer allowed to walk to school. The school run has become part of our culture. How much more danger is there of us being overprotective when we are in a strange environment which we have entered amidst dire warnings from friends and family of the dangers inherent in taking children into such a situation. A little dose of godly common sense is needed. Parents must take the natural precautions and trust in their heavenly Father for the rest, much as you do each time you wave your child goodbye and he/she goes out of your sight.

Maintaining a healthy family platform as described in chapter two is the best way of helping a child cope with stress. Marjory Foyle has said: 'The healthy platform is based on humble parents who recognise their own inadequacies, yet rely on the grace of God to give them what they need to rear their children.'

Values

For most families ministering overseas, service is a very prominent value. No-one is in it for the money or career enhancement. This then tends to be the value they pass on to their children. It is a good value but one which doesn't figure highly in the world to which they are returning. Ajith Fernando in his little book *The Authentic Servant* says:

> Christians from affluent countries may be losing their ability to live with inconvenience, stress and hardship, as there is more and more emphasis on comfort and convenience. Many are unable to stick with their commitments when the going gets tough.[1]

Returning TCKs pick up these vibes and often react very strongly to them. They are intolerant of such ease and affluence. They tend to be outspoken in defence of their adoptive countries where they may have seen much poverty and hardship. To be faced with such uncompromising views can be very uncomfortable and land the TCK outside the very society he wants to be part of.

The servant attitude is also influential when it comes to making career decisions. TCKs often look for jobs in the service industries; they are looking for creativity, not wealth; they are concerned about exploitation and open to being exploited themselves. Prior to re-entry they need to be made aware of the wider range of career opportunities open to them and helped to explore their gifts and preferences, being made aware that there are many areas of life to which they may have not had much exposure.

Home leave

There are many names for this now – home assignment, home ministry assignment (HMA) – everyone knows what it means and most people dread it. It refers to the time between assignments when the family comes home for a rest and refreshment (don't laugh!), opportunity to meet with supporters and sending churches, catch up on home life, have spiritual and maybe vocational refreshment – all in the matter of two to six months. Most families cannot wait to get back overseas after HMA for a rest!

When asked how she felt about HMA, one adult TCK replied thus:

> I hated it. I was made fun of for being 'different'.
> Academically and socially I was at least 3 years ahead of my peers. The weather was horrible. I was tired of living out of suitcases and smiling for strangers who all knew every minute detail of my life from my parents' slide shows.

For children, this can be an agonising time. They are leaving behind their friends and home, meeting a vast number of strangers, many of whom make patronising comments and want them to show off their linguistic skills or strange clothing. They have to sleep in a different bed every other night. The question which faces parents and agencies is, how can they reduce the stress of HMA?

Of course, there are lots of people to see and business to be conducted. But does it have to be a frantic round of visits, meetings and lack of privacy? Good planning well before the event, liaison between the family, the agency and the sending church can alleviate a lot of the stress. I recommend that planning should be started a year prior to HMA and should start off with a questionnaire requiring the family to address some of the issues ahead of time. The nearer anyone gets to departure the less likely they are to be able to make plans.

Firstly, there is a need to consider what the goals are for HMA:

- Where are you going to live?
- Does your child need time in a home country school?
- How many churches do you need to visit?
- Where are your supporters based?
- What are your plans for spiritual refreshment for yourselves?
- What Christian camps are there for your children?
- What about a holiday?
- Do you need any vocational training?
- What about an extended family reunion?
- Do you need to spend time at the agency's HQ?

When the answers to those questions have been sorted out, there is then a need to prioritise, to work out the possible from the probable and find out who is there to help and provide resources – this is where the bridges of chapter five demonstrate their usefulness.

The first question is the most important. Families need a base whilst they are home, somewhere that they can make their own and enjoy a reasonable degree of privacy. One family, having been on the move for three weeks in different people's homes, said to me, 'If we wanted to have a decent row we had to go out for a walk!' A base of some sort gives a child a sense of security. The best provider for such a base is the sending church. They have the means and personnel to search out what is available and the will to equip it. Of course, some families have their own homes to return to, but in many cases this is let out on a long-term lease and not available to them.

Secondly, if parents wish to put their children in to school for a short time, they need to give the school ample warning. If they have maintained a relationship with a local school and a link family, this will be a lot easier. It may be

'If we wanted a decent row, we had to go out for a walk.'

necessary to time HMA so that children are able to get an experience of mother-tongue schooling.

When it comes to visiting friends and supporters I recommend that, instead of parents trailing children round a dozen or more homes, they identify in advance some key geographical areas for supporters, and ask one group within that area to be responsible for inviting everyone living within, say, a fifty-mile radius to come to the supporter's home for a day to meet the family. Drinks can be provided, visitors encouraged to bring packed lunches, and it is possible to see thirty people for the effort of spending one day. Moreover, if it is in the home of someone known to the family, the children can be running around having fun with their long-lost friends while parents do the serious talking. It helps to have a couple of well-prepared coffee table books with photos and captions about the place where they have been working and digests on what they have been doing. This saves a lot of wear and tear on the family.

Churches and supporters also need to be educated about being sensitive with how they treat children. Many TCKs have to endure the agony of being paraded up front, dressed in national costume and asked embarrassing questions about what their parents are doing, particularly embarrassing if their father has been working in a sensitive area where his Christian identity was not spoken of. Johnny had returned with his parents from the Middle East and was hiding himself nicely at the back of the Sunday school class when the teacher said, 'OK, the Johnsons are back with us. Come up front Johnny and tell us all about what you've been doing.' Reluctantly, Johnny came forward and was asked 'What does your daddy do?' 'He's a water engineer,' he replied. 'Yes,' persisted the teacher, 'but what does he really do?' 'He mends pipes and things,' Johnny went on manfully. 'But we know what your father really does,' said the teacher, desperate to get him to use the m-word he'd been told never to use. What an ordeal.

Children may enjoy being involved in meetings and dressing up but it is important that they be consulted first and their permission granted before they are subjected to it. It is unlikely that adolescents will want to participate.

Finally, parents who are in a cross-cultural marriage need to ensure that it is possible for both parents to visit their home country, even if not every time. It may be that such a course of action is not open to them, but children need to be exposed to all of their cultural heritage if possible. It helps explain how mum or dad ticks. Agencies need, too, to plan this into their budgeting with a cross-cultural family.

Christian peers

In some situations, parents may feel their children are missing out on social interaction with Christian peers. They may be in isolated situations where there are not many Christians or there may be young people from very different backgrounds. How can they ensure their children are spiritually nurtured? There are some good Sunday school materials that families can receive from home to run their own classes, and in some cases it is possible to set up a pen-friend arrangement.

Parents need to discover what there is in the way of camps that their children can attend. I have already mentioned the value of doing this whilst on HMAs. There may be regional camps and gatherings to which you could send or take your child, even if you don't have much going on locally. Norway has been running specialised camps for some time now and in England there are many events which run special streams for children. Often they take place in the summer and are under canvas and therefore relatively cheap.

Information can be obtained from Christian magazines which friends could send overseas.

If there isn't much going on where you are serving, maybe you need to consider opening up your own home and becoming the focal point for work amongst children. Teens particularly need a place to meet, talk and have fun.

Finances

The issue of money, how much of it anyone should have, how it should be used, the standard of lifestyle to adopt, is a very tricky subject. It is the sort of thing that can lead to tension between team members on field. The gap between living standards in the States and many parts of Europe is considerable and it is quite a test of unity to be comfortable with one's own lifestyle without criticising or judging that of colleagues.

TCKs get used to a simpler lifestyle in many cases. They are privileged to see God providing for their needs. I view the year my husband spent at Bible college with no funds coming in and three children aged 3, 6 and 9 to support as having been a good experience in their lives. They do not have money worries, they have seen the proof of Paul's words, 'My God shall supply all your needs' (Philippians 4:19).

On the other hand it is easy to get into a very negative frame of mind as parents, to be always saying 'We can't afford that,' and to seem stingy. Parents need to have worked out their own attitudes to finances positively and biblically. Just because means are straitened doesn't mean one has to be negative. Knowing that your clothes are hand-me-downs or come from the charity shop doesn't have to make you feel deprived. Many people I know who are not in the 'living by faith' boat are very proud of their charity shop bargains.

Julia, who lived overseas from the age of 6 months until her return at 18 for tertiary education, was firstly an

MK then a TCK with the diplomatic corps. She comments: 'When I went to International School, there was the embarrassment of second-hand clothes and marmite sandwiches, when surrounded by kids whose drivers waited all day for them in air-conditioned BMWs.'

Children who have seen God provide and have lived by a budget cope much better when back at university than do their friends whose parents were always able to bail them out. They are far less likely to end up in serious debt. They do need, however, to be made aware of the cost of phone calls and emails which you may have previously financed but which falls on their shoulders once they are at college or living at home. The first bill can come as a nasty shock!

Spiritual growth

We all want to pass our faith on to our children. If we have held to the 'Family in Ministry' principle, they will have had the opportunity at first hand to see God at work, often in ways that would not have been possible had they stayed at home. Financial provision is one way, but safety, healing, paperwork permissions and people coming to faith will be others.

As part of the Family in Ministry, our children are encouraged to pray with and for their parents. It is important that these times of prayer are not just focused on the work and parental needs but start with the God for whom the whole family is there and include opportunity for the children to share their concerns and desires – whole family in ministry.

The following unsolicited comments from TCKs are very positive regarding their faith:

One of my positive experiences was to have been a part of a close community and family of Christians (age 11–13).

If you have lived in a Mediterranean lifestyle, you can understand certain passages of Scripture better.

It leaves room for strong personal identity with Christ and the church universal since other 'places of belonging' are weaker.

It challenges your Christian faith when you move.

You're not alone, talk to Jesus. He never changes and you'll need that security in the middle of change.

The people that have been important to me and their values have shown me a great way of living – the Christian life.

John White in his book *Parents in Pain* makes a point which I think all Christian parents need to take on board. Many have taken the words of Proverbs 22:6, 'Train a child in the way that he should go and when he is old he will not turn from it,' as a promise. If they bring their children up to follow Christ, then that is just what they will do. However, as White points out, Proverbs is just that, a book of sayings which recognises the general truth. In general, it is true that children follow the faith of their parents.

But it is not a promise. Each child has its own free will and is answerable for its own faith. We cannot make bargains with God. Some children choose not to follow the example, not because it was a bad example, but just because they feel it's not right for them then and there. It's one of the hardest things a Christian parent ever has to face and bear. But it is pointless castigating ourselves with guilt for what is not our responsibility. The question 'Where did we go wrong?' is futile.

Decisions need to be made under the hand of God, with love and consideration for the whole family, and the consequences are left in his hands. His love as a Father for our children is greater than anything we can feel. Listen to this TCK who was born and grew up in Japan till the age of

11, after which she boarded in England and spent holidays with her family:

> I never regret being a missionary kid. Occasionally, I might dwell on the hard times and be negative, but overall, I wouldn't want to be any different. I feel privileged to have been brought up in the way that I was. I always knew that my parents loved me, that they were doing what was right, trusting in God, and even on the other side of the world I knew that in a real sense they were always there for me. I have learnt a lot of lessons which I think has helped me to be mature, and be more independent, or rather more dependent on God. Change is something that I've learned to deal with (e.g. going away to university for me was not as scary, difficult as a lot of others found this). It's helped shape me into the person I am today and for that I am grateful to my parents and God. May they never give up on me, because I've still got a long way to go yet!

Education

No, not children's education but the education of local churches, sending agencies, extended families and supporters. Most of these do not really understand what it means to leave home and take a family overseas. The hardest time for families serving overseas is the time they return home. They need advocates with all the above and mentors to see them through the experience. If you have no-one to do that for you, then you need to start training someone. The material in this book is not just for you, it's for them too. So buy them a copy and make sure they read it and understand the nature of the TCK experience, the stages of transition, the pain of saying goodbye.

Jesus calls us in John 13 to be the servants of each other. That means being the servants of our children too. In John 15 he says, 'Greater love has no man than this, that he

lays down his life for his friends.' Ajith Fernando identifies as
first among the friends we die for, our family members.
Referring to Ephesians 5:25 he says, 'Most wives would say,
"I don't want my husband to die for me. Just tell him to talk
to me!" Talking when you are very tired is a kind of death.'

He goes on to say that some Christians fear that the
challenge he presents, to die for those we are called to work
with: our families, our churches and our mission fields, may
encourage people to live an unbalanced Christian life.

> They point to many who 'killed themselves' for the gospel
> but who in the process neglected their health and their
> families. They are now very disillusioned as they struggle with
> physical and spiritual burnout, bitter spouses, rebellious
> children and a sense of defeat at the end of their ministries.
> Indeed it is important for us to look after our health as
> Christianity is concerned with the physical aspects of life too.
> But I think the Bible does leave room for situations where we
> will suffer physically owing to our commitment.

He concludes with six features of biblical discipleship which
will enable us to fulfil our ministries well and without
disillusionment if we follow them as well as taking up the
cross.

- Have regular, unhurried time with God in prayer and
  Bible study.
- Guard the joy of the Lord.
- Take a Sabbath rest.
- Work with the body by delegating responsibilities to
  others without trying to meet every need.
- Sacrificially fulfil our responsibilities to our families.
- Look forward to the coming glory which enables us
  to live with frustration on earth.[1]

The following is an open letter written by a group of TCKs in Cyprus. I trust it will encourage parents; what they have to say is well worth listening to.

Hi,
What follows is a few reflections about our lives as TCKs. Some of us like our life and others don't so the comments are as varied as our experiences and feelings.

So we'll start with the good things and there are lots of these.

You have given us a varied and interesting foundation for life, which we appreciated the older we became. We star-rated many of the advantages as follows:

- making friends with many nationalities ★★★★★★★★★★
- having the opportunity to travel ★★★★★★★★★★
- getting to know a new culture ★★★★★★★
- appreciating different foods and sensory memories ★★★★★★★
- learning to speak another language ★★★★★
- enjoying the benefits of a variety of styles of education ★★★★★★
- seeing the benefit of our parents' work ★★★★★★★

But we did not all find it easy. Some of the harder things included:

- changing educational systems ★★★★★
- missing opportunities available in our home countries ★★★
- not having enough money ★★
- but especially with regard to friends, leaving, losing ★★★★★★★★
- and having to keep in touch ★★★★

Because we have the same capacity for feelings and emotions as you do, we know you can understand what moving may mean to us.

We would like to encourage you:

- to listen to us about anything we want to say
- to tell the whole truth about any move, e.g. the positive and negative
- to let us tell you what we feel, even if we express displeasure
- to help us adjust slowly, at our rate, into the new culture
- to help us to learn the local language if we are in an immersion situation
- to help us master our own mother tongue
- to encourage us to get a broad understanding of where we live
- to give us a positive picture of your culture so that it's easier for us to re-enter

Please don't be afraid to get us help if you see symptoms of struggle, maybe even professional if you think we need it.

Try not to refuse or to restrict exposure to or protect us unnecessarily from situations of danger (it's OK if you like bombs and the like!).

Don't worry about us unduly or stereotype us!

Thank you for everything. It may take us time to understand, so please keep listening. You're the only ones who have lived where we have lived.

Please pray for us and teach us to trust the love of God. Remember that we absorb your positive, patient spirit and your model of the Christian faith.

Thank you for listening!

Questions

1. List four priority areas in your life. How much time is spent on each? Are you a workaholic? Would you recognise symptoms of burnout?
2. What difficulties have you experienced in nurturing the spiritual growth of the family? What resources are there to help you? What practical steps can you take to make time for such nurturing?
3. Are there conflicts between ministry, lifestyle and family? Is it necessary to lay down some firm guidelines and limits? Are there national believers who can act as mediators in difficult situations?
4. How far do you involve your children in decision-making? Do they perceive guidance as inclusive of their needs and wishes?
5. What strategies do you have in place to deal with separation within the family, whether during short trips, boarding school, or tertiary education? How can you place a positive value on parental absence?
6. In a protected situation overseas, it may be easy to maintain and guard children's spiritual values and well-being. How do you prepare children to cope in a secular and hostile environment and to maintain their faith? What are the issues you anticipate them struggling with?

Note
1. 'The Authentic Servant' by Ajith Fernando, published by OMF.

 Appendix

A Summary of Normal Human Development

Dr Marjory F Foyle

This pattern is based on the model of development of personality by Erik Erikson who dealt with the development of the whole person, although he covered little spiritual material.

Erikson's model of development related to a series of normal life events called **Crises of Life**. At each stage something important has to be learnt called **The Task**. Serious failure to learn the task may have adverse effects on personality development. We must remember that none of us completely learns the developmental task, and this does not harm us in any way. Each task can therefore have a positive or negative result, but the usual is a ratio with the balance on positive.

Three problems arise when following Erikson's model:

1. The English language. 'He' may mean 'she' when talking of children. 'Mother' may mean 'Father' in modern circumstances. I have therefore often used the word 'carer' to cover for both house father or mother situations.

2. The different social structure of today as compared with Erikson's time. For example, no specific reference has been made to single parents, or to homosexual couples adopting children. However, today's social changes have not affected the actual events described under each crisis, only the accompanying relationships.

3. The ages of each stage. Today the stages begin earlier, but I have made no changes in Erikson's description. We need not be rigid about it.

Stage 1. Infancy. Birth–2 years

The task – trust versus mistrust

During this period basic trust is established, the trust capacity, but this is built on throughout life. It is learnt from caring parents.

There are four main parts to this crisis:

1. Birth. Causes a complete change of environment.

2. Feeding. Totally different from being fed through the cord. The child learns that needs will be met, but that gratification can be delayed. He begins to understand the difference between 'me' and 'not me'.

3. Teething. Two important things are learnt: compromise, and absence need not mean loss of basic trust.

4. Weaning. An experience of loss which is overcome by basic trust.

Signs that basic trust is developing satisfactorily

These vary from child to child, but some of the following will be present:

1. Thriving, shown by weight gain and general well-being. This is the most important sign.

2. Feeding and sleeping reasonably well.

3. Response to smiling faces as they appear.

4. Growing ability to let carer leave him for short periods of time.

5. Developing bowel pattern.

Remember that not all of these may occur: for example, the child can sleep well and feed poorly, or the reverse, without there being a serious problem.

Lack of trust will be indicated by remaining irritable or apathetic, failure to thrive (without physical cause), general failure to establish the rhythm of life at this stage. But remember that babies can regress to this stage if there is a prolonged change in their usual routine, and they recover once stability is restored. So do not get worried.

Stage 2. Early childhood. 2–4 years

The task – autonomy verses shame and doubt

This is the time of the 'terrible twos'. The big issue is 'who decides?' Independence develops as walking begins. Autonomy is accompanied by the development of self-esteem, through the following accomplishments:

1. Physical progress. Muscles can be used as the child wishes, enabling the child to run away from mother, to throw things or hit people, and generally to choose his own wishes rather than hers. Hence the temper tantrums if thwarted.

2. Toilet training. The child can now refuse to use the potty, but self-esteem increases if he does use it and is praised for it.

3. Social conflict. This is associated with walking and freedom to grab anything. The child learns how to be autonomous without upsetting others. He also learns that society demands some order by becoming rigid.

General advice

1. Try to avoid all but the essential confrontations, and remember it will all pass. Being difficult shows he is normal!

2. A little time alone in his room (with the door open) may be the best thing after a temper tantrum.

3. Try to keep the environment the same. This is the age of rigidity as the child controls his turbulent psyche by establishing sameness around him.

4. As he gets older give him small areas of control.

The end result is autonomy without causing problems to others, which produce shame and self-doubt. Earlier learning of basic trust and the importance of compromise is further strengthened.

Stage 3. The play age. 5–7 years

The task – initiative versus guilt

The child learns how to take the initiative while keeping within acceptable boundaries, and thus avoiding personal guilt. Certain major things happen during this stage:

1. Enjoyment of adventure. He makes his own friends, goes off exploring, climbing trees and swinging vigorously etc. He returns to parents at longer intervals of time, but still needs reassurance.

2. Understanding absence. In earlier stages, if something was absent it had gone, disappeared, and was never coming back.

Now the child knows that absence means temporary loss, not abandonment.

3. Learning discipline. He learns where he can do things, and where he cannot. He likes things clear-cut, hence rules help at this point. He learns that if rules are broken he incurs displeasure, though not loss of love.

   Family love teaches of the goodness of God and of humans.

   Family discipline teaches of order, justice and fairness. It should never be over-rigid and inflexible.

   Do not fear you will fail the child. If he knows he matters to you and you will support him and love him, then you have succeeded. It is good to apologise to him when you goof things up! He then knows you are human and the relationship becomes closer.

4. Language develops. The supreme age of asking questions, although this begins much earlier. Growing reading skills plus further development of the personality are behind the barrage of questions. If you don't know, tell him so, and this increases his understanding of you as a separate human being.

5. Fantasy runs wild. Imagination is the way of harnessing the huge amount of mental energy that is released at this time. It is so plentiful the child really thinks

for a time that his fantasy is true. He will learn to distinguish between pretending and reality fairly quickly.

6. The social circle enlarges. Teachers and friends become very important. Adequate support is needed. Discuss with the child where he goes to school.

7. Genital interests develop. Pleasure is centred initially on the mouth, then on power and control, and in this stage it settles on the genitals and the difference between the sexes. This is not sexual as in adult sexuality, but expressed as curiosity. Early sex education is helpful in developing sexual understanding without guilt. Attachment to the parent of the opposite sex occurs, again usually non-sexual, but as a preparation for future cross-gender relationships.

Stage 4. The school age. 6–12 years

The task - industry verses inferiority

This stage is called the latent period, energy concentrating on social relationships, academic learning and physical growth, rather than on major psychological changes. The big change is that the child attempts to master the environment by adjusting to it, whereas in an earlier stage he tried to change the environment by screaming and temper tantrums.

Modern children will, however, only adjust to the

current environment to a certain extent. For example, they will accept the educational curriculum but not the destruction of the rainforests.

Major concern - learning how to do things

1. Acquiring practical skills. Being industrious. This also involves status at school and whether academic subjects are status-worthy or not.

2. Acquiring social skills. This involves fitting in, and understanding the local pecking order - there are local distinctions made between people. It can be difficult for MKs or TCKs to understand this on returning home.

Special problems of the school age

1. Inferiority, the opposite of successful industry. This can develop to the point where he feels he will never be good at anything, and he withdraws from society.

2. Unwise efforts to solve the problem.
   - Giving presents to other children to earn their friendship. He may steal to do so.
   - Giving in to peer pressure to do something the parents do not approve of.
   - Overwork and over-conformity to earn teachers' approval.

The help parents can give

1. Provide a harmonious and secure background.

2. Prepare for this stage by establishing lines of communication from an early age. Talk and pray together.

3. Teach the child some skill at which he can shine.

4. Ensure adequate playtime, reduce home pressures on the child.

5. Discuss active bullying with the school.

Stage 5. Adolescence. 13–19 years approx.

The task – identity versus identity diffusion

This stage is concerned with finding adult identity. Personality development accomplished so far begins to disintegrate, with brief recapitulation of previous stages. Confusion is the main ingredient. The goal is to reintegrate the adult personality.

Three special characteristics of the adolescent group

1. Leadership. Frequently a pop star or a sports personality is the most important person.

2. Language. A group language develops, incomprehensible to adults!

3. Uniform.

The causes of personality disintegration

1. Biological:
   - Changes in the body
   - Changes in body image
   - New turbulent sexual feelings.

2. Social Demands by parents, peers and teachers.

3. Psychological Demands. The adolescent must answer the question 'Who am I?' Methods of resolving the identity crisis:
   - Acting out the conflict.
   - Endless conversations.
   - Transient identifications.
   - Spiritual experimentation.
   - Practising the working role.

Managing the adolescent (watch and pray, it *will* pass!)

1. Preparation:
   - Guard basic trust, communication skills, togetherness of the family.
   - Give sound spiritual education, regular and devoid of pressure.
   - Give ample early education on drugs, sex, and the problems they may face, in an unthreatening way.

2. Coping with the adolescent:
   - Keep the home framework regular, secure, and happy. Be seen to be fair, and in agreement about management.
   - Recognise and respect the emerging adult. Provide as much freedom as possible, with clear boundaries. Be available for talking.
   - Check that rules are sufficiently adult.
   - Maintain loving patience with clothing, make-up etc.
   - Stay patient with emotional changeableness, but do not let it impact on all of you the whole time.
   - Open your home to the gang.
   - Harness the huge physical energy.
   - Be patient with hyperoccupation of the bathroom – have a rota!

Development of Personality

STAGE	AGE	TASKS TO BE LEARNED	RESULTS OF INADEQUATE LEARNING	IMPORTANT PERSONS
I	Birth – 2 years	Basic trust	Mistrust	Mother
II	2 – 4 years	Autonomy	Shame and doubt	Mother and Father
III	4 – 6 years	Taking initiative	Guilt	Parents of the opposite sex
IV	6 – 12 years	Industry	Inferiority	Peers, teachers, parents
V	13 – 19 years	Personal identity	Identity diffusion	Everybody
VI	20 – 30 years	Social intimacy	Isolation	Husband, wife, friends
VII	30 – 65 years	Social responsibility	Self-absorption	Family and society
VIII	65 – death	Integrity	Despair	Family and society

Families on the Move

▶ Further Reading

The Third Culture Kid Experience by David Pollock and Ruth Van Reken, published by Intercultural Press, Maine, USA 1999.

Life Story Work, published by British Agencies for Adoption and Fostering, London 1999; a booklet suggesting ways to make a life story book with children.

... and Bees Make Honey, edited by Jill and Roger Dyer, published by MK Merrimna, Kingswood, Australia, 1995; an anthology of TCK writings.

Scamps, Scholars and Saints, published by MK Merrimna, Kingswood, Australia, 1991; another anthology by the same editors.

A Country Far Away, by Nigel Gray, published by Andersen Press, London, 1998: a comparison of life overseas and life at home, with illustrations, written for children.

Harold and Stanley say Goodbye, by Jill Dyer, published by MK Merrimna, Kingswood, Australia, 1998; a storybook for young children about moving.

The Berenstain Bears Moving Day, by S. Berenstain, published by Random House Trade, USA, 1981 (3-8 yrs).

When Grover moved to Sesame Street, by J. Stevenson, published by Golden Press, USA, 1985 (3-8 yrs).

When Africa was Home, by K.L. Williams, published by Orchard Books, New York, 1991 (8-12 yrs).

Sojourners: The Family on the Move, by R. & S. Rowen, published by Associates of Urbanus, USA, 1990.

The Growth and Development of Children, by Catherine Lee, published by Longmans, Harlow, 1999.

From Birth to Five Years, by Mary D. Sheridan, published by Nelson, London, 1993.

Entertaining and Educating Your Pre-school Child, by Gee and Meredith, published by Usborne, 1987.

Creative Play, by Dorothy Einon, published by Penguin, London, 1986.

Infant Projects, Subscription Department, Scholastic Publications Ltd, Leamington Spa; a bi-monthly teacher's magazine with pictures, posters and projects for children aged 4-8.

Junior Focus; as above but geared to 8-12 year olds.

Don't Pig out on Junk Food, by Alma Daugherty Gordon, published by EMIS, Wheaton, USA, 1993; a TCK's guide to survival in the US.

Travel with Children, by Maureen Wheeler, Lonely Planet Travel Guide, Victoria, Australia, 1995.

Festive Allsorts, by Nicola Currie, published by Church House Publishing, London, 1994; ideas for celebrating the Christian Year.

A Feast of Seasons, by Margot Hodson, published by Monarch Books, London, 2000.

Re-entry: Making the Transition from Missions to Life at Home, by Peter Jordan, published by YWAM Publishing, Seattle, USA, 1992.

Re-entry: A Book of Readings, published by Abilene Christian University, Texas, USA.

From Birth to Starting School, by Dr Richard Woolfson; published by Caring Books, 1997, quoted in the Daily Telegraph, 9th October 1999.

Raising Resilient MKs: resources for Caregivers, Parents and Teachers, edited by Joyce M. Bowers; published by the Association of Christian Schools International, Colorado Springs, 1998.

Hidden Immigrants: Legacies of Growing up Abroad, published by Cross-Cultural Publications, Indiana, USA, 1997.